All you have to be is Light

MARANATHA

All You Have to Be Is Light

By the Holy Spirit and Maranatha

ISBN: 979-8-9871742-0-3 (Paperback)

Biblical references and quotations include the use of the following versions: NLT (New Living Translation), KJV (King James' Version), CSB (Christian Standard Bible), MSG (The Message Translation), AMP (Amplified Version), ESV (English Standard Version), NIV (New International Version) and The Voice.

First printing edition 2022.

Onefirm Media Corp.
PO Box 186
New York, NY 10031

Dedication

To my Abba, Yeshua & Helper, and my dad, through whom God sent me this gift of writing and a way with words.

And Amanda, who believed in this book before it became a book.

And Mr. K, who kept me grounded all the times I got overwhelmed.

Prayer

Ephesians 1:18 (The Voice): *'Open the eyes of their hearts, and let the light of Your truth flood in. Shine Your light on the hope You are calling them to embrace. Reveal to them the glorious riches You are preparing as their inheritance.'*

The light from this book leaps from its pages into your eyes. You will begin to see like you have never seen before. You will see what God is seeing, what He has been trying to show you.

—

'THIS IS A KIND OF KNOWLEDGE THAT COMES WITH FERVOUR. THE ZEAL OF THE LORD WILL DO IT.'

Table of Content

Introduction

22/01/2022

I have always known I would write a book. I have always known. I also always thought that my first book would be about me. It's not. It's another story of His rescue; of the one apart from the 99. Of His mercy.

If you are saved, you should save others; this is the core of evangelism and is a responsibility for every Christian. The gospel must be shared but where do you start from? How do you go from not being able to speak up about Jesus: stuttering and shaking when you have to; or not even contemplating it because of fear to not just preaching the Gospel but fully living it to the extent that you even share it without speaking?

That can be your life. You can be all that God has called you to be, without being confused or scared or having to shift with every new tide that flows in. Imagine you, as a Light-bringer, carrying light wherever you go - with men being drawn to that light and getting saved because of it. Imagine being irresistible because of the

Holy Spirit at work in you; imagine your presence has - in its company - beauty, wisdom, answers and…LIGHT.

Truth be told, many believers have a shallow idea of who they are and the power and authority they have to really impact this world. This, in turn, affects how they spread or do not spread the Gospel. Christians often think of evangelism as a straightforward thing - and it is - but it goes deeper than that. Evangelism is not just telling people about Jesus but also about living full lives as a result of this knowledge in you.

If you have also ever wondered why or if personal development is important for you as a Christian, then this book is for you. Why do you have to look or sound good? Why do you have to exercise? Why do you need to speak well? Why do you need to be knowledgeable on a vast range of topics? How do these things help you spread the Gospel? The answers - to these questions - which you need are in this book!

All you have to be is Light explores the theme of 'Disconnection,' a major hindrance to evangelism and a common phenomenon in the lives of many believers. The Disconnect involves bringing certain aspects of our lives to God and shielding other parts from Him. As a final solution, this book connects the dots while laying out practical guidelines on evangelism that actually work, replete with the author's real-life experiences.

This book will teach you how to share Jesus with those around you *by just living up to your true potential.* In the end, you do not have to be tall or short, shockingly handsome or plain Jane, charismatic or conservative—no; all you have to be is Light. The kind God has called you to be; when this Light shines, men will find their way to God through you.

You are that Light! But the question persists, 'where do you start from?'

This book will show you not only *where*, but *how*.

The Light Journal

When the Holy Spirit and I finished writing this Light book, I felt poured out. What Abba and I made was ready to be delivered into the hands of many, to change lives. But something was missing... something that is now tangible in your hands.

Unlike many other books you may have read, *All You Have To Be Is Light* is written in a very practical fashion. This means that you get to start applying these tips and making the necessary changes in your life as you go along with reading. As an avid reader, I know that it's very easy to forget priceless gems harvested from books when you do not write them down as you read. The best time to do this is as you take in information so that they actually stick. Writing things down makes them more concrete and achievable. If you cannot be accountable to your own words, how can you be accountable to anyone else's? You should do things because you said you would do them: Your. Word. Is. Enough.

To ensure this, after each chapter is a journal section where you get to pour out your thoughts about what you have read and add action steps on how you can start working towards them. This journal is divided into sections based on the book's chapters. Each section is divided into several parts where you get to answer important questions and take notes as well.

Additionally, I have provided affirmations from the Word to help you confess the Word of God in your life concerning each section. I've found these reminders to be very helpful in my own devotional life.

I did not write this book for you to skim through, no. I want you to take your time to follow each line of text and see all the places that you can fix up in your life. With this journal, you will begin to take definitive steps to becoming not just a better version of yourself but also a light--bearer who gives light to others. You will begin to be conscious of the burning light within you and take steps to spread that light to everyone around you through everything that you do or say. Jesus will be so proud of you.

I beg you, bring honesty along with you within these leaves. The truth, the truth is ready to set you free. Can you hear? The chains are clanging on the cold hard ground.

I cannot wait for who you will become. The world cannot wait either. Come, let's get started.

— Maranatha. The Holy Spirit says hi.

Flip the page.

1

My Burden for the Lost

W̲e're talking about beginnings, I feel obliged to start from mine, where it all began.

06/09/2021

I wake up feeling heavy and with tears in my eyes. It is a bit confusing and as I search through my memory for fading fragments of a forgotten dream, I find none. I feel like my heart is crushing within me but it makes no sense to me...

Why was I crying?

I knelt to pray. As I did, a Scripture came to mind, and a light bulb came on in my head. It was from **Matthew 9: 35-38 (NLT)**:

35 'Jesus travelled through all the towns and villages of that area, teaching in the synagogues and

announcing the Good News about the Kingdom. And he healed every kind of disease and illness.

36 When he saw the crowds, he had COMPASSION on them because they were confused and helpless, like sheep without a shepherd.

37 He said to his disciples, "The harvest is great, but the workers are few.

38 So pray to the Lord who is in charge of the harvest; ask him to send more workers into his fields.'

The focus is on **verse 36**, the confused and helpless crowd, like sheep without a shepherd. These were the ones I wept for, for the people who lived the life that I used to live. A life where God was anywhere else but at the centre.

It was sometime later when I came across Benny Hinn's *Good Morning Holy Spirit* that I knew what had happened to me that morning. I had a taste of the Burden for the lost souls. This is an experience that imitates the sorrow the Holy Spirit feels when we hurt Him.

> It is 'the heaviness of grief' turning 'into a burden for lost souls that I had never felt before.'
> - Benny Hinn

Benny Hinn described this grief as 'an oppressive, heavy load of grief'; further describing it in this way:

'...the Spirit of the Father's heart is breaking with the needs of mankind. Perhaps for those weeks, He allowed me a glimpse of His agony for the lost. When you have felt the pain that the Holy Ghost feels; it clings to your consciousness and will never leave you.'

- Benny Hinn's Good Morning Holy Spirit

God's heart was daily breaking for lost souls and for once, I felt it. That morning I prayed so hard but the only words that came out of my mouth were, 'SEND ME,' 'GIVE ME MEN' instead of my usual petition for my family's financial breakthrough. It paled in comparison to this urgent matter in my heart. For the first time, I realised what it really meant to *seek God first*. I realised there was so much more to fellowshipping with God than asking over and over for my material needs; after all, God already knew what I needed before I asked and those things would happen in due time.

Lives were being lost. People were living empty, pouring out nothing from nothing. People were so lost.

And THAT is why the Gospel must be shared.

The Ministry of The Holy Spirit

...is evangelical. It is the Holy Spirit who convicts the world of sin (**John 16:8**), convincing the sinner of their need for Christ to lead them to reconciliation with the Father.

When I first became a believer, all I wanted to share was the Good News. By the Spirit's leading, which He confirmed to me after a fast on the 13th of September 2021 through a close friend; I knew this was my calling in life. To bring people to Jesus first and everything else second.

But how?

Like many Christians, I had a straightforward idea of what evangelism was or should be. I tell A, B, C to Z about Jesus, back it up with stark Scriptures and voila! Like magic, they would see reason to be with Jesus.

I mean, even I did not become a believer in that way.

This book you are reading was born from a mini project of mine called 40 Days, and I will share with you in succeeding paragraphs how that started.

23/11/2021

It had been 4 months since I returned from the university. Returning home as a believer was new to me; I had left here in January as a *'Christian because my parents are Christians'* and I was back saved and having true knowledge of the Gospel. My family, especially my father who was a pastor, absolutely loved it because it usually felt like he was the only one that really understood this Christianity thing. *Nobody else too send.*[1]

---

[1] This is a Nigerian Pidgin phrase for ***everyone else was carefree with it.***

However, I was used to being by myself in school so it was new. Being with my family, who had experienced a bulk of my bad behaviours as an unbeliever was also very testing because I felt the pressure to act like the old Favour they knew. Sometimes it felt like I was two people. But more on that later.

Many times, I felt stressed out and choked up by being at home. That I worked from home did not help. I would not say I was depressed but if I wasn't, then I was almost there.

Here is an entry from my journal:

> *"Every Monday, my laptop eyes me wearily but triumphantly, like a mother eyes a child who returns to eat the food he rejected."*

I was slowly starting to look like a vagabond, as well; I never went out so I paid less and less attention to my looks. This morning, I remember feeling like I had swallowed dust that refused to follow the normal digestion process.

It was on this day that I felt a spark again. My Walk of Faith had been full of ups and downs. On some days, my feelings were all over the place, and I wanted to do so much for God; on other days, only my knowledge of God carried me from one day to the next. Here's a melancholic poem I wrote on one of such days:

> *Some days are filled with ecstatic exuberance*
> *Other days carry a quiet energy that wishes not to be disturbed*
> *On some days, we want to speak and be heard*

On other days we will not utter a sound, for the thoughts in
our heads are loud enough
On some days, we move
On other days we stay
On some days, we live
And every other day we don't, we die.

On this same day which was the start of something new -
although I did not know at the time - I also remembered the burden and heaviness which choked my throat and squeezed my heart
that first morning in September. I cannot say what catalysed it but
as I remembered, I bowed deep in guilt; I knew I had been slacking
on my promise to Abba. I had let the worries of the world weigh
me down. I was asking God for things when He wanted to give
me people.

As I prayed, my heart began to shift once more to that spot
God wanted me to be in order to carry out His will (there is a
heart-position you must have before you can carry out the will of
God; *a position of willingness*) and that was all I needed to move
from where I was (immersed in my perception of financial and
material lack) to where God wanted me to be - a true soldier in
His army.

By the time I was done praying, a plan had formed in my mind.
That is the thing about prayer: whenever I talk to God, the instructions are right there in front of me always. *As sure as seashells on a*
shore after a wave.

And why not? **1 John 5:14 & 15 (CSB)** lets us know that:

14 'This is the confidence we have before Him: If we ask anything according to His will, He hears us.

15 And we know that if He hears whatever we ask, we know that we have what we have asked of Him.'

40 DAYS

The 40 Days Project inspired by the Holy Spirit was to kickstart my evangelical ministry. I was to talk to 40 people for 40 days about Jesus Christ. Seems easy, right? Ha-ha, not when you consider that I was a chronic introvert who worked from home—meaning that I was literally and figuratively married to my laptop and by extension, the internet.

So, I did what I could. I talked to people online; It made a lot of sense since that was where I woke up, ate and slept.

You see, *I could not afford to see any obstacles when God had clearly shown me what to do.*

As a natural melancholy, I was organised to my teeth, so I drew out a structure for my project. I headed to my WhatsApp, started from the people closest to me (because I was more invested in the people I was closest to. I mean, I would really like to see these ones in Heaven!). Then went further to my course mates from the university and other acquaintances.

I had several methods I used to start a conversation, like:

1. **Do you think you are a good person?** Then I would go on to have a conversation about how the human standard of 'good' was flawed and how we could not be good without God. Besides, being good was not enough, man's inherent nature of sin due to Adam's disobedience made it impossible to truly be good. If being good was enough, God would not have sent Peter to preach the gospel to Cornelius **(Acts 10)**.

2. **What do you think happens after you die?** The eternity conversation was always a good provocation but it almost always ended in an *'agree to disagree'* manner which I absolutely HATED. Maybe this sounds a tad aggressive but I was to blame. My mistake with this tactic was expecting a certain honest response from people. I thought it was obvious that Heaven was the goal. However, questions like this often threaten to reveal people's deepest fears along with questions that they don't have an answer to. The result of this was that many people answered the question 'dishonestly' and I did not know where to go from there so it felt like a loss for me. *Every single time.*

3. **Would you do a Bible plan with me?** YouVersion[2] is THE bomb, really. Many people were actually open to taking a plan with me and I would try to discern

---

[2] YouVersion is an online and mobile Bible platform published for Android, iOS, Windows Phone, and many other operating platforms. In 2022, according to YouVersion, its Bible App features 2,759 Bible versions in 1,831 languages, audio Bibles, offline capabilities, as well as over 800 Bible plans and devotionals.

(from what I knew about them) what topic they would be more responsive to; faith, loss, stress etc.

4. **How do I know you believe in God?** This question is for those who claim to know and believe in Jesus. The charge here is to perform actions consistent with their beliefs. I usually cite **John 14:15 (KJV), "If ye love me, keep my commandments."**

5. **Would you like me to pray for you?** This was always a yes.

Follow up proved very helpful. I would always go back and check up on them in some way, taking a cue from Apostle Paul, here, either by praying for them or just popping 'by' to say 'hi.'

As I write the first draft of this manuscript, it's the second week of March and I only finished talking to these 40 people last week but come back, come back, that is not the point I am trying to make here - the Holy Spirit did His work, I was only slower in doing mine (*covers face in shame*). But I did it.

Those 40 Days (which actually spanned over 3 months because sometimes, I would have to speak with one person for more than a day) gave me practical experience that no theory could have helped me even imagine. I did talk to over 40 people in that time, and that interaction fed my desire to write this book. I noticed several classes of people to whom I preached to:

1. People who have been looking for a catalyst in their faith walk. I became a sort of faith walk mentor to quite a few of these ones.

2. People who seemed to know the truth but had no desire to pursue it. They appreciated my prayers but made no move to proceed in faith.

3. People who were sure I had ulterior motives for talking to them. I mean, may *God punish the devil*[3] *who made you so wary of love brother Dave.*

4. People who had questions but did not want answers. These people acted like they wanted answers to questions like, *'why do good people die and bad people live,'* but when I actually answered these questions - their irresponsibility was exposed and they had no excuse. I use the word 'irresponsibility' because these people blamed their non-belief in God on these questions that supposedly did not have answers. However, getting these answers did not change anything either. So, they went back to search for harder questions to ask people they were sure could not answer it. *They were not ready for the truth.*

The list goes on but number 4 is another reason why I am writing this book; many Christians exist that cannot answer the simplest questions about Christianity. To an extent, this book will teach you, as a believer, how to answer some of these objections

---

[3] In a fit of controlled anger, this phrase could be an Nigerian Expression for wishing judgement upon the devil - not the human being - responsible for the misfortune/misconception in question.

because it is important to know how to defend your faith so you are not shaken by questions that actually have answers. Believe me, every question has an answer if you are willing to search for it.

The 40 Days Project shook me, made me happy and made me feel crazy at some point too. Being exposed to the thought processes of people felt like a sojourn into unknown territories: some people thought eternity was a farce, some people thought it was just a way to control people and make them subservient. *This Gospel that had healed my life? That changed me?* At several points, I withdrew because how can you talk about MY Word of God like that? I got angry. Severely, I backed out to catch my breath because I started to feel overwhelmed too.

However, I learnt something which many people get wrong in evangelism that I will share with you now. Like many other Christians, I saw evangelism as a checklist I had to tick every day. *'Tell Dave about Jesus...done.' 'Tell Joshua about Jesus...done.'* What? It was not enough and I did not know that so I ended up frustrated and sad. I will not say it was totally ineffective; the Word of God is powerful like that and for those with open hearts, they received Jesus. However, I was not so effective because I did not know any better.

Why are these people not listening to me? Why could they not see what I was seeing?

First of all, if it was that easy, why did it take me 21 years to become born again?

This is the work of the Holy Spirit.

My first mistake was trying to convince people instead of actually preaching to them. By default, I loved to read and know stuff so trust me when I say I always had an answer and if I did not, I looked for it and found it. I soon found out that that was not enough because sometimes, the things of God often cross the borders of logic. The Bible tells us how the wisdom of God is like foolishness to men **(1 Corinthians 1:25; 3:19)**.

In reality, only the Holy Spirit can convict an unbeliever of sin. This is why He is the ultimate evangelist.

John 16:8 (NLT):

8 'And when he comes, he will convict the world of its sin, and of God's righteousness, and of the coming judgement.

9 The world's sin is that it refuses to believe in me.'

So, you see, I was reaching in my role when my role was to reach out (using some certain principles that I will teach you in this book) and afterward, seal up with persistent prayer.

That was when I started to pray for them. Every night, I would mention the names of every person I had spoken to and ask God to make their mistakes lead them to Him. The more I thought about my life before Christ, the more I became convinced that I would fail if I tried to make anyone believe in God. It was simply beyond my power. I, too, thought I knew it all before I met God. I, too, was not willing to answer questions about where I might end up after death.

I, too, used to think that Heaven did not really matter and if it did, hellfire may be more fun. The more I contemplated my life before Christ, the more compassion I started to have for unbelievers.

I made many mistakes in becoming the evangelist that God called me to be and that may have slowed me down but it did not stop me. I knew I would write this book to help Christians move from the shallow idea of evangelism to how and what it is really supposed to be.

But I slacked again. Months passed. I had school issues to resolve. I had work. As a chronic multitasker, I had problems concentrating on single tasks for long periods. Also, I had never written a book before so it was a bit overwhelming to think about. But God did His thing again.

25/02/2022

It's early this morning. I wake up, pray and towards the end of my devotion, an image of a book flashes in my mind, unprovoked. I remember my 'abandoned' project and sigh on how I have slacked...again.

I sit for a while to clear my head before checking my phone to see several missed calls from my close friend, Faith. I return the call, and you will not believe the first thing this girl said:

'I think you should write a book, Favour.'

Here was God reminding me again of a task at hand; I felt guilty, but mostly humbled. It was so spot on that I also felt like I was seeing stars. And by the time you are done with this book, so will you.

Turn the page and let's get started, enough with the introduction.

2

The Disconnect

3 **John 1:2 (NKJV)** - *'Beloved, I pray that you may prosper in ALL THINGS and be in health, just as your soul prospers.'*

When I became born again, something changed within me. I knew the kind of life I wanted to live; I knew how my former life had fallen way below the standard of God for me; in fact, it had left the room. But guess what? I became new because of Jesus.

However, I unconsciously fed from a long history of Nigerian religious conservatism that advocated for long-sleeved shirts and even longer skirts. I felt that I had to be a certain way, look a certain way, act a certain way; because I was a Christian.

I am sure that this has happened to many Christians. In an online Christian meeting where I was invited to speak, a majority of the questions revolved around what manner of dressing or appearance (especially trousers) was appropriate for Christian girls. It was saddening that such questions which had been trending since I was a little child still remained unanswered.

The answer is quite simple.

1 Corinthians 10:31; (CSB):

'... **whatever you do, do everything for the glory of God.**'

But maybe it is still not this simple. I, for one, unconsciously began to withdraw into myself, neglecting many aspects of my personal life because I was now a servant of the Lord. Did God ask me to? NO. I'll give you examples; I became more interested in preaching the Word of God and less interested in much else. That fervour was expected, God really changed my life, but along the line it deteriorated into a laxity in many other areas.

I did not care about how I looked - which was certainly not the case before I got saved. I did not care about what I wore. I did not care about being the best possible version of myself. All that mattered was the Word. But was this even in the Word? That you forsake certain parts of your life and appreciate other parts? If there is one thing that I now know about the Word, it is that it goes 360 degrees and touches on every part of our lives. I got this wrong at the beginning of my Walk of Faith.

But you do not have to and with this book, you will learn how.

Introducing, 'The disconnect.'

The disconnect represents the divide that exists subconsciously in the mind of the Christian and works to separate aspects of their lives, presenting it like some parts should be given to God and others shielded from Him because they do not concern Him or because there seems to be no distinct connection to God. This is a big hindrance to evangelism for how can you preach a Gospel that you cannot live?

It is everywhere, the disconnect: in communication and interaction with people, in wellbeing, work and more. Many Christians fail to realise that every part of life connects back to God. That asides everything working together for your good because you love God, everything in your life should also work together to give God glory.

Let us examine this Scripture together, it may be familiar to you.

Romans 12:1 - 2 (MSG):

'So here's what I want you to do, God helping you: Take your everyday, ordinary life—your sleeping, eating, going-to-work, and walking-around life—and place it before God as an offering. Embracing what God does for you is the best thing you can do for him.

Don't become so well-adjusted to your culture that you fit into it without even thinking. Instead, fix your attention on God. You'll be changed from the inside out. Readily recognize what he wants from you, and quickly respond to it. Unlike the culture around you, always dragging you down to its level of immaturity, God brings the best out of you, develops well-formed maturity in you.'

Just look at that! I will be dissecting various parts of this verse for a better understanding of the message I am trying to pass across:

1. **God helping you** - The most important thing that you need to know is that you WILL fail if you try to do any of these or ANYTHING at all, without God's help.
2. **Take your everyday, ordinary life** - Take everything that you do, everything, and give it to God. Take your waking up, your sleeping, how you brush your teeth, your standing and sitting and let EVERYTHING be an offering before God. Let nothing be left out.
3. **Embracing what God does for you is the best thing you can do for Him** - This is your true worship! It is taking all that God has given to you and giving it back to Him. It is accepting all God's blessings in all aspects of your life, connecting all the dots and finding out how it all relates back to Him. That is how to embrace it. Like the servant who was given 5 talents and went to invest it to make 5 more **(Matthew 25:14-30)**; embracing what God has given us shows how we improve on each and give it back to Him.
4. **Don't become so well-adjusted to your culture that you fit into it without even thinking** - This is the trap many Christians fall into! They become born again and their spirit man comes alive as connected to the Holy Spirit. But they forget that the flesh has become adjusted to the pattern of the world due to consistent influence from a source other than God. They forget that the flesh

needs to be brought under the control of the Holy Spirit. So, they continue doing the things that they used to do or adopt a laid down tradition without questioning it because it has become a habit. Guess what though? Bad habits can be replaced with the Word of God and by the Power of the Holy Spirit **(2 Timothy 3:16)**, you have the wisdom to replace destructive habits with God-centred ones. **2 Timothy 3:16 (NLT)** says **'All SCRIPTURE is inspired by God and is useful to TEACH US WHAT IS TRUE and to MAKE US REALIZE WHAT IS WRONG IN OUR LIVES. It CORRECTS us when we are wrong and TEACHES us to do what is right.'**

5. **Instead, fix your attention on God. You'll be changed from the inside out** - This is it! This is everything. You do not change habits by trying to change them, you do so by shifting your focus to God. For it is **'God…working in you, giving you the desire and the power to do what pleases him.' (Philippians 2:13 NLT).**

6. **Readily recognize what He wants from you, and quickly respond to it** - This is what should be on your tongue every morning. *'Dearest Abba, how can I please You today?'* Consider **2 Timothy 2:4 (NLT)** that says, **'Soldiers don't get tied up in the affairs of civilian life, for then they cannot please the officer who enlisted them.'** As a soldier in God's army, your primary business is God's business. No soldier wakes up thinking of what to eat or what to wear etc. They have only one uniform, their camouflage. Just like you have only one uniform

which is the armour of God **(Ephesians 6:11)**. You put that on every morning and you go out representing the Father, the Lord of the Angel Armies.

7. **Unlike the culture around you, always dragging you down to its level of immaturity, God brings the best out of you, develops well-formed maturity in you** - Do you realise that the spiritual maturity you seek to attain cannot be found in the world? The world is so petty, it can barely figure out what it is doing. And this is not surprising, considering the tyranny of the one it is under. The devil is not one to want or desire anything good - he perverts all that is good and covers it with a 'gold-plating.' So, you think you have the good stuff from him but all you have is like a wolf in lamb's clothing; one day, the skin will drop to the ground. 'Gold-plated' can never quite be gold: with time it will show. But God? God will bring out the best in you; He will refine you to gold. **John 15:2 (NLT) says 'He (God)...prunes the branches that...bear fruit so they will produce even more.'** God wants the very best for you and the amazing thing about this is that He does not leave you to grow or develop by yourself, He continues to prune and refine you to be the best that you can be—by His Spirit.

If anything, the Scriptures teach you how to live a FULL life by giving every aspect of it to God.

Having examined these Scriptures, it is obvious that Christians need to realise that when they proclaim God as the *God of all*, their actions must reflect it. For example, you love the omnipresence of God because it means that you will never be in danger as He sees you always. Ha-ha. But what about when you are being a glutton and insist on having more food than you can finish? You think He does not see you when you give less than you should at work? You think He is not so concerned with your bad sleeping habits as long as you are passionate about soul-saving?

Now wrap all those thoughts and the like, stand up, head to your toilet and dump them in the bowl; press the flusher and let them go into the soakaway where they belong. God introduced Himself to Hagar as 'the God who sees!' (**Genesis 16:7-14**).

That should give you shivers. Hagar was a powerless slave - subject to the will of her masters. She had no say in what happened to her, of course she must have wondered if there was someone, somewhere, who was witnessing the injustice that had happened to her and God shows up and says, 'YES. I SEE YOU.'

He sees everything and yes, He IS concerned. More concerned about you, your well-being and every aspect of your life. Is He not your Father?

Every part of your life should evangelise, it works hand in hand with you preaching the Word verbally.

Matthew 5:16 (CSB) goes,

'In the same way, let your light shine before others, so that they may see your good works and give glory to your Father in Heaven.'

Trust me, 70% of the time that people will come across you, you may NOT be preaching the Gospel (and that is if you even preach at all *rolls eyes*), unless, of course, that is your ministry or designation. You may be eating; you may be sleeping; you may be at work; you may be chatting; you may even just be walking or passing by. In these times, will the Word still be evident in you? Or is it only when you are shouting, *'the kingdom of heaven is at hand?'* **Will people know that you are a Christian if you do not speak?**

Moving forward, I will present 6 aspects of life which are very important but often get disconnected from God because the connection is sometimes not apparent and even when it is, it is trivialised. The disconnect is not limited to these six but with these ones, I will prove to you that everything else connects.

I pray, from the depth of my heart, that you get this message which the Holy Spirit wants to pass across to you. May these words penetrate your heart and find a home in it—in Jesus' Name. Amen.

Journal prompt:

Go over the term of disconnection over and over in your mind. Is there any part of your life that you feel is currently separate from God? Write down the things that come to your mind, so you can start working on them as you follow the question prompts to begin your journey of discovering Light. May the Spirit guide you to His truth.

Romans 12:1- 2 (MSG):

'So here's what I want you to do, God helping you: Take your everyday, ordinary life—your sleeping, eating, going-to-work, and walking-around life—and place it before God as an offering. Embracing what God does for you is the best thing you can do for him.

Confession: I declare and agree that every part of my life is fully given to God. No aspect of my life is left out of the wonderful workings of the Holy Spirit - in all that I do. I am set apart and fully consecrated - everything that makes me, me - for the work God has purposed me for—in Jesus' Name. Amen.

Take this as the beginning of your story. At this point you must have read chapters 1 and 2 of the book. What are your expectations? What parts of your life do you think are disconnected or not in tune with God? What is the reason for this? How can you fix it?

_____

_____

_____

_____

_____

_____

_____

_____

_____

_____

_____

_____

_____

_____

_____

_____

_____

_____

_____

3

Food and Evangelism

1 Corinthians 10:31 (CSB) - *'So whatever you eat or drink, or whatever you don't, do everything for the glory of God.'*

You do not need a magician, or me, to tell you that overeating or under-eating does not give God glory. Or wait, did you not know that eating is something that can and should give God glory?

Poor eating habits are such an *in-thing* these days. I am guilty, too; I have tried to under-eat as a method of watching my weight and *oh-how-disastrous* that was. In 2019, for the first time since 2016, I drastically lost weight because of the intense stress and depression I suffered for several reasons back then in university.

In fact, everybody else noticed before I did but when I finally did, it was like a dream come true! I had been trying to lose what seemed like my *'baby weight'* for the longest time so I grabbed this opportunity with both arms - and legs. However, I wanted to maintain it the wrong way, not by eating healthy and exercising, but by starving myself appropriately and sometimes not eating at all. It would make me crampy and angry but I NEVER related the negative feelings to my malnutrition.

We commonly say that a *hungry man is an angry man, but many* people do not even realise that they are constantly in *not-so-good* moods because they do not feed properly. Malnutrition is not just undereating. A quick Google search defines it as a '*lack of proper nutrition, caused by not having enough to eat, not eating enough of the right things, or being unable to use the food that one does eat.*' In essence, when your body does not get what it needs - not what you think it needs – it becomes an issue. Psychological studies have shown how hunger negatively impacts mental function:

> Hunger impacts emotions, judgments, and behaviours because it impairs self-regulation. In this view, hunger releases the constraints that typically keep people from feeling unbridled emotions, making impulsive judgments, or aggressing against others. This regulatory depletion hypothesis was first inspired by work demonstrating that mental effort can deplete blood glucose. Thus, it is assumed that negative, high arousal emotions or outbursts of aggression when hungry occur because individuals cannot regulate their feelings without sufficient blood glucose.
>
> - MacCormack & Lindquist (2018).[4]

---

[4] MacCormack J. & Lindquist K. (2018) - *Feeling Hangry? When Hunger is Conceptualized as Emotion. https://www.researchgate.net/publication/325694374_ Feeling_Hangry_When_Hunger_Is_Conceptualized_as_Emotion*

You need FOOD. Drinking water is not left out, too, and it has many benefits: once I started being intentional about being hydrated, it contributed to making my skin better in my battle with acne.

The truth is, Christians do not often connect the fact that eating well glorifies God; Exercising, drinking enough water, treating your body (God's temple) like a palace that it is. Not overworking yourself; sleeping and resting well. Taking breaks when you have to. Only recently, I realised that a constant dry lip issue I had was not because of my 'ineffective' lip gloss but because I was constantly dehydrated. Now I always have a water bottle beside me.

Do you know? That many bad tempers and anger issues can be traced to a lack of food, too? I cannot count how many times good food puts me in a good mood *(ha-ha, see what I did there? Entering the studio soon *wink*)*

Let's take it to the Bible now - Remember Elijah? What did God do first after his complaints? Elijah slept (rest) then God fed him and gave him water.

1 Kings 19:4 - 9 (NIV):

4 'While he himself went on a day's journey into the wilderness. He came to a broom bush, sat down under it and prayed that he might die. "I have had enough, Lord," he said. "Take my life; I am no better than my ancestors."

5 Then he lay down under the bush and fell asleep. All at once an angel touched him and said, "Get up and eat."

6 He looked around, and there by his head was some bread baked over hot coals, and a jar of water. He ate and drank and then lay down again.

7 The angel of the Lord came back a second time and touched him and said, "Get up and eat, for the journey is too much for you."

8 So he got up and ate and drank. Strengthened by that food, he travelled forty days and forty nights until he reached Horeb, the mountain of God.

9 There he went into a cave and spent the night.'

Twice he was fed, because the journey ahead was lengthy. It was not beyond God to propel Elijah on spiritual fuel but hear this, why would He do that when He already made food for that purpose? It is like expecting God to think for you; why did He give you a brain then? In fact, what Elijah could do after eating the meal (travelling for forty days and nights) was still supernatural! But…God worked that through the regular!

Physical needs must be met first, or else, it may hinder your general functioning—including the spiritual aspects. **The physical affects the mental, and the mental affects the spiritual.** That the Holy Spirit is involved does not mean that you should be ignorant of the things you must do or put in place. Wisdom is profitable. If you lack it, ask for it; **James 1:5** confirms this.

What are your eating habits like? Are you eating once or twice a day or only when you're hungry? Do you eat junk with a sprinkle of food (guilty as charged but repentant in Jesus' Name. Amen). Or you cannot even remember the last time you ate a fruit? Is fast food your best friend? That is dangerous. Sometimes, that crankiness that you feel, getting funny ideas or that sudden mood swing that has no immediate reason may be because you have not eaten properly. Hunger can give rise to some very funny ideas you normally would not give your audience if you were well-fed. You need to prioritise your feeding to prevent unnecessary temptation or sin.

It is God that gave us these foods, a surplus of them.

Genesis 1:29 (NIV):

' Then God said, "I give you every seed-bearing plant on the face of the whole earth and every tree that has fruit with seed in it. They will be yours for food.'

Yet, we cannot throw moderation out of the window. There are two shows I always head for when I take charge of the DSTV remote; Nickelodeon's *SpongeBob Squarepants* (please do not raise your eyebrows) and TLC's *My 600 lb life*. The latter chronicles the experiences of people with a bodyweight of over 600 pounds who are forced to make drastic lifestyle changes in order to reduce their weight or face dire consequences. I always ask myself the same question, *'how can somebody eat to the point where they cannot walk for 2 minutes without feeling agonising pain?'*

The torture on their faces were very evident, many would break down uncontrollably because they could not believe how they got to that point. Maybe it was like a detached or out-of-body experience for them? I do not know, but what was evident was that their bodies were suffering greatly because of too much food. And they could not do anything else because of it: not work, not hobbies - some even had to have a family member take care of their personal hygiene like bathing. How sad.

Now, that is an extreme physical case, but there are also emotional consequences. For example, when you use food as a coping mechanism, here is what happens:

> Many people use food as a coping mechanism to deal with such feelings as stress, boredom or anxiety, or even to prolong feelings of joy. While this may help in the short term, eating to soothe and ease your feelings often leads to regret and guilt, and can even increase the negative feelings. You aren't actually coping with the problem causing the stress. Further, your self-image may suffer as you gain weight, or you may experience other undesired effects on your health, such as elevated blood sugars, cholesterol levels or blood pressure.
>
> - Cleveland Clinic[5]

Using food as a coping mechanism means that you learn a lot less about how to actually solve your problems, which is a very

---

[5] Cleveland Clinic - https://my.clevelandclinic.org/health/articles/10681-the-psychology-of-eating

important life skill that you need in order to go far. Food or any-thing else as a coping mechanism is only effective in the short term.

I implore you to use food for what it was meant for. Eat slowly and intentionally; food should be savoured and every flavour uncovered by your tastebuds - it is such an experience, being mindful as you eat. **Many prayer points would be avoided if you take good care of yourself through food.** Eat the right things, food is the fuel that your body needs to survive. Eat at the right time—heavy food or any food at 1:00 am is certainly not included. Trust me, your body will thank you for it. So will your spirit.

Action point

Make changes to your diet, it may be hard but you can choose to be intentional about it. It is not a thing of joy to *'not know how to eat'* or to *'eat so little.'* It WILL affect you in more ways than I have mentioned here. Don't wait to be hungry before you eat, eat when you should because your body needs fuel. Be intentional about what you eat too. Don't let the only vegetables you eat be the ones inside your burger. Take lots of fruits, too.

You have heard that *you are what you eat.* This is true because when you eat properly and regularly, the good effects are more prominent than any kind of skin care. Protect and take care of this body that God has given you, let it shine. Your body can preach too, let it shine. When you take care of your body, you take care of God's property as a good steward of His temple. Be a proper caretaker of God's temple and you can be a proper evangelist, too.

Journal prompt:

Take a minute to reflect on what you just read; what dropped into your mind as you read through this chapter? What changes do you need to make regarding your eating habits and hygiene? Follow the question prompts to find your answers.

1 Corinthians 10:31 (CSB):

'So whatever you eat or drink, or whatever you dont, do everything for the glory of God.'

Confession: My eating habits please God, immensely, and I give glory to God with my appetite. My tongue will not crave things that will harm my body and I will take care of God's temple through food in the right manner—in Jesus' Name. Amen.

Are there areas that need improvement in your feeding? What changes can you make to do better? Write out your starting steps.

   "From now on, I will…

_____

_____

_____

_____

_____

_____

_____

_____

_____

_____

_____

_____

_____

_____

_____

_____

_____

_____

_____

_____

_____

_____

4

Physical Appearance and Evangelism

1 Peter 3: 3 & 4 (NIV) - *'Your beauty should not come from outward adornment, such as elaborate hairstyles and the wearing of gold jewellery or fine clothes. Rather, it should be that of your inner self, the unfading beauty of a gentle and quiet spirit, which is of great worth in God's sight.'*

This Scripture has put many people, including me, in real trouble. Here is a Word that tells us to focus on inner beauty which is of great worth in the sight of God. But, point me to where it says to neglect physical appearances? It does not.

Imagine you are presented with a crowd of people and asked to pick one person out of many, who would you pick? Chances are, you would pick a person who appeals to your physical senses in one way or more. There is absolutely nothing wrong with that because while inner beauty exists, it is not obvious at first impression so you can barely make a choice as a result of it. This inner beauty, as related by the above Scripture, is for your relationship with God first; with man, your outer beauty often comes first. Many times, people - even after perceiving inner beauty - still opt for that physical appearance because of how charming it can be. I remember crushing on many human species of the opposite sex when I was a teenager and even as an adult but there was no one - NOT EVEN ONE - who was not a good-looking person in a way—at least to me.

This is not to say that some people are *ugly*, it is to say that everyone has a physical appeal to them which must be played up. Not all tastes may appeal to you but you would know when a person looks good or not; that is what I am talking about! How can you think that because you serve God, your appearance does not matter? That is some shallow way of thinking.

You cannot wear ill-fitting clothes because God looks at the heart. Well, Man does not and cannot. And guess who needs saving? Man.

How do you look when you enter a place? How do you walk? Do you have bad posture? Working from home had me sitting at a desk for major hours of the day and it took me becoming conscious of that to begin to adjust and sit properly so I do not slouch or experience back pain in my old age because I will be needing to throw my grandkids in the air and catch them. #Respectfully.

Once, I was at the airport and I looked to my left and saw a man sitting with his legs thrown wide apart. It was not so beautiful to look at; it communicated to me a sort of reckless abandon that was not meant for public display.

These things matter: etiquette and table manners, your appearance, how you smell, your walking or sitting posture, composure - everything about your physical appearance says something about your carefulness or negligence down to your toenails. In a video clip or book - I cannot remember the exact medium - Pastor E. A. Adeboye related how he was at a dinner with reputable men and threw etiquette out the window by filling his mouth up with food; no pausing, just gobbling down the delicious meal. Unfortunately for him, his host asked him a question at the wrong moment and he could not answer because his mouth was filled to the brim. Crazy coincidence, right? But that can happen to anyone and the consequences may be costly.

The Word calls us to live like citizens of Heaven (**Philippians 1:27**); like royalty! If God be a king, then you, His child, must be an heir and joint-heirs with Christ (**Romans 8:16-18**). What do you think of when you see kings or queens? Dignity! There is a manner in which you must carry yourself because you are royalty.

I told you in the first part of this book, how getting saved made me withdraw into a sort of shell where nothing mattered but me preaching the Gospel verbally. This often happens with people who were living at extremes before they received salvation. For example, I've noticed that the dressing of most ladies who used to dress somewhat indecently before receiving salvation would change drastically, also to an extreme bordering on carefreeness, after being born again.

I believe the idea is to distance themselves as much as possible from that old way of living. It's quite understandable, but there must be a balance. Nollywood has had a lot of fun with this concept: a girl who used to be wayward becomes born again and suddenly the skirt cannot fit if it is not toe length. Also, her Bible becomes fixed to her chest, she can never put it down. Nothing is inherently wrong with these things, however, the stereotype is what needs to be stopped. Why? It puts Christians in a box! We are much more than what we choose to wear or not wear.

Before I got serious with God, I was not so much of a dress-up person in the first place, *but I try sha*[6]—if I do say so myself. However, I had always prioritised my smart and bookish nature over my appearance, so that did not change even after I got saved.

Here is the point I am trying to make and one thing you must know - that being born again does not mean that you become a new being physically. Everything you were before, you will need to sanctify with God's truth in order to change them. Who you were before getting saved - habits and all - is the same you'll be afterwards. It takes training and subjecting your flesh to the influence of the Spirit in order to change.

> 'You may get saved in an instant, but the change happens over time.'
>
> - Larry Brey[7]

For example, my 'bookwormish' nature is the reason that I love to study God's Word so intensely; that's just me. A person who is not naturally a reader may find it more difficult. However, it is no excuse for stagnation. You can focus on God's word and do better. A

---

[6] *I did okay*

[7] Larry Brey: *Between two Extremes* https://www.youtube.com/watch?v=xCW5YHYxdtk

very close friend of mine, Emma, who has an amazing fashion sense (and ALWAYS looks good - I don't know how!), told me how she started to dress up more and post on social media without being so bothered about having the perfect pictures. This was because of the confidence that being in Christ gave her and her realisation of the role that she had to play as being a part of the body of Christ. I felt so proud. That's it! That's how it should be! You are a Representative of Christ.

My friend, these things are important. When I started to work out, I worried about being vain and focused on the things of the flesh. You may be thinking that it's focusing on the wrong things but it's not. A friend of mine told me about how his dad fell ill and the doctor said it was something that could have been avoided if he was physically active in his younger days. You do not want to look like 50 when you are 30 - TAKE CARE OF YOUR PHYSICAL APPEARANCE.

When I became consistent with exercising, it cured me of the chronic fatigue that I used to have. Isn't it funny? That you actually feel tired because you're not physically exerting yourself and you feel stronger and agile when you do? Funny thing. Working out does wonders for your mood and confidence level, too - not to mention that it gives you a great body (you do know that your body is 50% of what makes a great outfit, right?)

Black - or any other skin colour - *don't crack* is nice to say, but it is not for negligent people. It takes work, caution, and consistency. Be careful about your physical health; being responsive to your body and knowing when something is not right is crucial so you can take action; not pushing your body beyond its capacity is important, so you do not break down. Sadly, Nigeria, my country, does not boast of a great healthcare system that lets Nigerians be conscious of their health status, but you can try. The first step is actually to have it in mind.

It is not a thing of joy to be lackadaisical about these things in your young age because you think you have time - you will never get away with it. Your young age should be a time of investment, not recklessness. A proverb of Solomon comes to mind whenever I think of doing something reckless because I am young. It's found in **Ecclesiastes 11:9 (NLT):**

> **'Young people, it's wonderful to be young! Enjoy every minute of it. Do everything you want to do; take it all in. But remember that you must give an account to God for everything you do.'**

If two evangelists approached you with the same word of God but one looks better dressed and physically attractive than the other; I'm not asking you, you would most probably go for the better look-ing one. Why? There is an appeal we all look for in people, some-thing that catches the eye. This is why it is important that we do not move by sight alone because it is often manipulated to achieve a desired result - it has been working since the days of old and it still works.

People steadily complain about people that overdress to events but guess what? They are the ones that get all the attention EVERY TIME and guess again? If they are selling something, people WILL buy it.

A paragraph in Robert Greene's *48 Laws of Power* goes:

'What draws attention draws power. We cannot keep our eyes off the audacious - we cannot wait to see their next bold move.'

See, you must recognise and understand the primacy of sight among the senses. What we see holds such power compared to what we hear or feel. In fact, sight is one sense that often convinces us the quickest. I'll give you a quick example: the way I read is a bit photographic which means I capture details as I see them. While this is great for storing information, if I capture the wrong information - NOTHING can convince me about what I believe my eyes have seen (*my friends will one day beat me up because of this; they can never manage to convince me once I am certain of something I saw*). I'm sure many people can relate to this. The eyes are powerful; even the Bible confirms this severally.

In **Matthew 6:22-23 (NLT),** Jesus teaches that **'Your eye is like a lamp that provides light for your body. When your eye is healthy, your whole body is filled with light. But when your eye is unhealthy, your whole body is filled with darkness.'** This communicates the potency of the influence of the things that you SEE on your mind, your psyche, your spirit, your body and you, as a whole. *What people see* influences them greatly, you can utilise this knowledge for evangelism by ensuring that you are not only a voice communicating God's eternal love for His children by calling them to reconciliation, but also a pleasant sight to behold. When you look good and presentable, people are more likely and willing to hear the Gospel you want to preach.

So, put some lipstick on. Get a nice haircut. Smile more and if you think that is tacky, practise a good resting face so you don't always look like you are ready for a fight. Wear makeup; don't be lazy about your appearance because you may be naturally beautiful; in my opinion *'nothing's fine that cannot be finer'*. Be intentional about it - is it going to be hot when you head out? Take a face towel with you. Does your face get oily quickly? Take some powder along. You actually become more stressed when you get stressed out and you know that you do not look so good; your confidence wanes too.

Etiquette

Since I wrote a bit about physical comportment, I want to add a bit more on etiquette. Etiquette is a necessity, especially in this time and age when some people feel it is okay to go to other people's houses, unannounced. Learn etiquette in eating, visiting people, how to sit, how to address people politely; use your earphones when you are not alone so you don't disturb others, speak quietly etc. There are many materials on this online; getting to know them is free. Your time is a small price to pay for the embarrassment you will be saved from by knowing these things.

My point is this: ***If you are light, act like it***. Shine bright. Your actions should be worthy of emulation. With Christ you have inner beauty, already, now let it show on your outside. This too will draw people to you, and they will know that your source is Christ.

Action point

Start being intentional. Every morning, I look at myself and examine my reflection in the mirror. Doing this helps me to be self-aware and know if one thing has changed in my body from the previous night. Know your body better than anyone else; you know you break out in sweat easily, find an antiperspirant that lasts longer. Use a good perfume. Find your scent. Learn table manners. Don't slouch. Learn good posture.

Be intentional about your physical health. Don't hold your pee. Stop biting your fingernails. Wash your hands as often as you can. Trim your toenails. Wear fitting clothes. Invest in skincare, it's not for females only. Know what fits you; play up your best parts - nobody is perfect - the ones that you think are have just found their pretty parts and are great at highlighting it. Some parts of you are perfect truth be told; let people see them and nothing else will matter. People always play up their good parts so you don't notice much else. It's not about being trendy or following the latest fashion, it's about always looking good. Style does transcend trends.

Be aware. Some people think that they only have to act a certain way when they are in public, but the truth is that charity begins at home. The result of this kind of thinking is that one day, you may forget yourself in public and heavy embarrassment may be your portion. Home may be your comfort zone but it is also your training ground.

Play up your best physical parts. This will involve many trials and errors but the best time to start is now. I am rooting for you!

P.S - This should go without saying but I am still going to say it—playing up your best features is no advocacy for indecency.

Journal prompt:

Take a moment to reflect on what you just read. How can you describe your dress sense? Are there parts that come to your mind which need fixing?

1 Peter 3: 3 & 4 (NIV):

'Your beauty should not come from outward adornment, such as elaborate hairstyles and the wearing of gold jewellery or fine clothes. Rather, it should be that of your inner self, the unfading beauty of a gentle and quiet spirit, which is of great worth in God's sight.'

Confession: I declare that I prepare the way for the Spirit to work in me and others around me through my physical appearance. Men will respond to Your light within me and my appearance will not deflect that light. Abba, I give You glory with how I look, all day and every day—in Jesus' Name. Amen.

Are there areas that need improvement in your physical appearance?
What changes can you make to do better? Write out your starting steps.

_____

_____

_____

_____

_____

_____

_____

_____

_____

_____

_____

_____

_____

_____

_____

_____

_____

_____

_____

_____

_____

_____

_____

5

Work and Evangelism

olossians 3:23 (NLT) - *'Work willingly at whatever you do, as though you were working for the Lord rather than for people.'*

I have worked since I got out of secondary school. By default, meaningful work has always been of interest to me - I give the credit to my parents who are pretty conscientious people themselves. Perhaps, this is why my dad gets scared that I would become so career-oriented and not want to start a family (this was a famous line I used to threaten my parents when I was younger. My mother's panic was quite hilarious to behold).

Now this habit formed most of my work life as I always looked for something to do. In 2015 right after my WASSCE[8], I assisted my

---

[8] West African Senior School Certificate Examination

aunt at her provisions store; right after I failed my first UTME[9], I got another job as a blogger for an entertainment website right up until I gained admission in 2016. Working in my previous employment sparked my desire to own my own website and I started Rehdwolf. com in 2016 right up until 2021 where I did some remodelling and it became www.Natha.ng.

I have said all that just to say, if there is one thing that has stood me out and continues to stand me out, it is my diligence at work. I will admit that I fall out of line, too; but mostly, God has really helped me be that person that can be reliable and dependable even to the point of making sacrifices where necessary. I have found, time and time again, that it pays.

Always find something to do. In the parable of the talents, I used to find this verse obnoxious:

Matthew 25:29 (NIV):

29 'For whoever has will be given more, and they will have an abundance. Whoever does not have, even what they have will be taken from them.'

Why would more be given to the ones that already have? I have gotten to understand that it is because of this: PROOF OF EXCEL-LENCE. You would rather invest in a person who has successfully

---

[9] Unified Tertiary Matriculation Examination

pulled off successful investments than someone who has no track record. In the work setting, too, people are more willing to assign tasks to you when they see that you already have something you are doing and you're managing it well.

In essence, maybe you have not gotten the job you want or the business you want to start; but there must be something you can start to give your CV a boost. There must be something that people can use to evaluate your capabilities. You must have and hone the skill of adding value to whatever it is that you do. Never stay idle.

While I do not advocate being busy just for the sake of it, it is true that *an idle mind is the devil's workshop.* Consider the story of the man in the Bible that gets delivered of demons and remains empty, causing even more demons than before to find a resting place within him **(Matthew 12:43)**. Like my pastor, Apostle Emmanuel Iren says, *'Nature abhors a vacuum.'*

Do you know? That God, through work, can bring to you people that you may never meet in church?

Matthew 9:37 (NLT):

36 'When he saw the crowds, he had compassion on them because they were confused and helpless, like sheep without a shepherd.

37 He said to his disciples, "The harvest is great, but the workers are few.

38 So pray to the Lord who is in charge of the harvest; ask him to send more workers into his fields.'

Where do you think the harvest is taking place? In your church alone? Among the brethren who already believe? The harvest is all around you but you cannot limit yourself to your comfort zone! There is a demand for the Gospel. It will help you to realise that Christianity is quite a popular religion so there are many people who want to know about it but have not found the right avenue to do so. Many people are searching for the right answers that you can give. Sure, there are many who will reject you and your Message, but there are many others who want to hear it. How will you get to those who want to hear the Good News if you don't pass through those who don't?

Work, the exchange of value whether in a formal or informal setting, forms the bulk of our daily interactions and as a believer, you must use every opportunity to your advantage—to shine your light.

Through meaningful work, what your hands find to do, you give glory to God:

Consider Genesis 2:15 (NLT) -

'The Lord God took the man and put him in the Garden of Eden to work it and take care of it.'

I have heard arguments about how 'work' was a result of the curse due to man's disobedience but guess what...the above verse was *before* the fall of Adam. God created the earth and He put man in charge of it to WORK on it and TAKE CARE of it. So even before man was cursed in this way: '...**cursed is the ground because of**

you; through painful toil you will eat food from it all the days of your life.' (Genesis 3:17 NIV), he was still charged by God to work.

I remember how my diligence at work got me my first laptop; not a penny of mine went into it. In the same way, I have gotten loads of favours from people I have worked with because of this trait. My point is this: in life, *nothing goes for nothing*. There is constant exchange of value through and through. Just like you are reading this book after purchasing it because of the information you believe it will impart in you; men will often show you favour from their perception of the value they feel you can impart them with.

When I first got saved, one thing that really prevented me from coming into the full embrace of God's grace was that I could not believe that all I had to do was accept it. Because of this perverted view of grace which comes as a result of sin and is what is at work in all humanity from Adam, we believe that there is something we must do to stay in God's good graces simply because society all around us believes in this norm of 'nothing goes for nothing', and over time, it is the culture that has prevailed. It is still a culture that cannot be ignored, value is important. Apostle Paul puts work in a perspective I love; he says in **2 Thessalonians 3:10 (NLT):**

'If anyone isn't willing to work, he should not eat.'

Now, this is by no means an advocacy for 'suffering' because I have found that many people equate 'suffering' with 'working'. The two are not the same. Work is simply an activity, according to Google, that is done *'to achieve a purpose or result.'* I must add; a purpose that is in line with God's Will. You do not want to succeed in a place where you are not supposed to be.

Another angle we must examine is 'attitude to work'. I talked about how my reliability found me favours with people that I worked with; this was simply because of my diligent attitude at work and my willingness to go out of my way even in situations where I would have been justified if I had decided not to. I have seen arguments on social media about people who refuse to go outside their work description and while it can be tricky because of how some employers actually take employees for granted, promotion rarely occurs within a strict performance of job roles. In fact, I have never seen it happen. People always want to work with people who prove that when the situation calls for it, they can show up even when it is not convenient for them. If you were an employer, forget salary, you would want the same kind of people around you or working for you.

Let me tell you a secret that many do not know: doing more at work, solving problems, going the extra mile is how you negotiate for promotion and a better pay within a good work environment - not a toxic work where it may be taken advantage of. It proves that you are ready to move beyond where you currently are. **While others may see it as *doing too much*, it is simply you making a way for yourself while others stick strictly to their job description and a status quo that can never get them noticed because the status quo is bland and made to blend.** When you fit in, you disappear. Read that again.

Work Ethic is important. Showing up is important. Diligence at work is important; whether you work for yourself or another. Ask yourself and answer honestly, what is your character like at work? Are you reliable or dependable? Would people rather have Plans A to X than have only you as Plan A? Do you always go past your deadlines? Are you an African timer - always late instead of early?

Let's look to the Bible, the source of all. Remember David? Saul's servant had a resume to give Saul when recommending him to the service of the king.

1 Samuel 16:18 (NIV):

'One of the servants answered, "I have seen a son of Jesse of Bethlehem who knows how to play the lyre. He is a brave man and a warrior. He speaks well and is a fine-looking man. And the Lord is with him.'

This CV is spot-on! Talent, check. Diligence, check. Communication, check. Appearance, check!

Your diligence at work will attract people to you. If a person can speak highly of you concerning your work, it reveals a whole lot about the kind of person you are. It shows that you are trustworthy, respectable and take the work of others seriously. That is worthy to have for a child of God!

Though many workplaces may not have a Christian culture, there is still a lot to learn in terms of organisation and how to build systems that will last for generations especially if you desire to carve a space for yourself within that industry. Many secular industries have hacked the mountains of influence on a scale that their Christian counterparts have not yet reached. It may seem sad but it is the truth. This is not a charge to copy-and-paste the same practices as the secular world when doing Kingdom businesses but competitor analysis is a crucial part of any marketing strategy for good reason. You must know how the other side is doing it.

Also, who is to say that you cannot bring God to your workplace? Many Christians leave their Christianity at home like it is a part of them that is separate, it is NOT. If the Bible tells us to work like we are working for God, then our work means even more than we think it does. It is an avenue for God to bless you; through your work and through people. It is your chance to influence your workplace for Jesus in little or big ways. By world's standards, the staff that tops the charts usually arouses the suspicions of others that something fishy may be going on in the background: deception, lechery and all sorts of evil to wade to the top. You can be that person that has God going in your background and even foreground when people examine you and your achievements! You can be proof that you can do it right with God.

1 Thessalonians 4:11-12 (NLT) says:

"Make it your goal to live a quiet life, minding your own business and working with your hands, just as we instructed you before. Then people who are not believers will respect the way you live, and you will not need to depend on others."

Would you look at that, by working in a way that pleases God, even unbelievers will respect the way you live. By being independent and being able to provide for yourself by the work of your hands, people will want to be around you because your presence becomes valuable. The benefits are endless! Work is for you. Do it.

In the same vein, do not become so work-oriented that you forget God, the centre of it all. The idea of *work-life* balance is a flawed one because there is just one life—one that revolves around Abba. Amen?

•••

If you work from home, here is an excerpt for you from my blog, Natha.ng

All my struggles of working from home: 14/03/2022:

Always do what you're supposed to do: If you live with your family, this is sooo important. If you have chores, do them early; if you have any other responsibilities, carry them out before you are reminded; contribute in some way to the upkeep of the house; take breaks; have a chit chat with whoever is home so it does not feel like you are absent when you are present. The truth is that you may find your work valuable, but that does not always translate to value for those around you unless you present a form of value they appreciate like giving them your time or money. If fingers are ever pointed, you will be acquitted.

Action point

If you do not have work, then find one to do. It will help you grow and that interaction with people working towards one common goal will teach you a lot that will help you even in church and your walk with God.

Have you been slacking at work? Fix up and do better. Set goals and achieve them. Become valuable at work so you're indispensable: your conviction will be taken seriously. Be the light at work. Don't leave Jesus at home, take Him to work with you. There's often strife and raised tensions in an office environment, Jesus is who you need to properly interact in a way that lessens this. Above all, God is your real boss; let this show in the quality of your work. Give it your best.

Be the light at work.

Journal prompt:

Take a moment to internalise all you just read. What comes to your mind that needs some fixing? What changes can you start making right now when it comes to your work?

Colossians 3:23 (NLT) -

'Work willingly at whatever you do, as though you were working for the Lord rather than for people.'

Confession: Lord, I accept the work you have purposed me for. I work willingly with my hands and I excel at everything that I set my mind to do. Men will see my work and know that I have a God. Above all, my work will give you glory and push the Gospel to the ends of the earth—in Jesus' Name. Amen.

Are there areas that need improvement in your work? What changes can you make to do better? Write out your starting steps.

6

Communication and Evangelism

Proverbs 15:23 (NLT)- *'Everyone enjoys a fitting reply; it is wonderful to say the right thing at the right time!'*

This is one of my favourite proverbs because of how apt it is! From 2016 to 2021, I studied Mass Communication at the University of Nigeria, Nsukka, but I do not believe any lecture described communication as succinctly as the verse above. No disrespect to my able lecturers. *Ahem.*

It is much more than sending messages and getting feedback from a recipient, it involves being intentional about it like King Solomon said.

Communication is life, and life is communication. I believe you must have heard before that everything you do or do not do is communication - it always sends a message. Do you know? That the things people see you do or not do, pass a message? A friend once told me that he thought I did not have a father because I never or rarely spoke about my dad to him. Now that is extreme but it is still communication!

Consider **Psalms 19**, where King David lauds the creation and how they declare the glory of God. I would definitely pass out and never wake up if one day the sky developed lips and started to sing *'Baba Baba Baba o!*[10]' one day but guess what, they communicate that God is King by just being!

Psalms 19:1-4 (NIV):

1 'The heavens declare the glory of God; the skies proclaim the work of his hands.

2 Day after day they pour forth speech; night after night they reveal knowledge.

3 They have no speech, they use no words; no sound is heard from them.

4 Yet their voice goes out into all the earth, their words to the ends of the world.'

Many people are not conscious of this truth which is why they do not take care to ensure that they communicate properly through all they do or say. That used to be me, too! (Still is sometimes but I'm learning *biko*)[11]. My friend, Amanda, used to complain about

---

[10] an indigenous worship song in Yoruba language. The first line loosely translates as 'Father, Father, Father o!'

[11] Igbo Word for *please*

how my lips would say one thing but my face would say a different thing; my expression and words were mismatched and would often result in miscommunication. This is a communication problem that many people have but don't bother fixing because *'it's just who I am. I cannot help it.'* Ha-ha, you can! Do you know what this lack of communication does? It makes you a liar because who can trust a person whose lips say one thing and their eyes a different thing? Not me. Not you either.

It takes practice. Stand in front of a mirror and speak, notice your facial expressions. Ask a close friend to keep tabs on you as well especially when you are out. Slowly, you will alter your expressions and make them correspond with your speech.

How can you lack social skills as a child of God? How can you be rude to people? How can you act like one that has no manners? How can you not care what people think? Apostle Paul says in **1 Corinthians 8:13** not to eat certain foods if it will make your brother sin, that is…caring what people think! How can you not think of the message people will take away from your actions? Don't you know? That as a Christian, unbelievers may be on the lookout for your actions in a bid to point out your faults? How can you not be cautious?

Some people are only nice to people in the church, people with the same faith or people who they think can help them and they do it to the point where they become obsequious. If you only talk nice to people who you can gain from, just like loving only people that love you, what makes you different from pagans?

Matthew 5:43-48 (NIV):

43 'You have heard that it was said, 'Love your neighbour and hate your enemy.

44 But I tell you, love your enemies and pray for those who persecute you,

45 that you may be children of your Father in heaven. He causes his sun to rise on the evil and the good, and sends rain on the righteous and the unrighteous.

46 If you love those who love you, what reward will you get? Are not even the tax collectors doing that?

47 And if you greet only your own people, what are you doing more than others? Do not even pagans do that?

48 Be perfect, therefore, as your heavenly Father is perfect.'

Let me show you something the Scripture points out that is very important in our communication;

Romans 12:16 (NLT):

'Live in harmony with each other. Don't be too proud to enjoy the company of ordinary people. And don't think you know it all.'

Enjoy the company of ordinary people! People you feel are beneath you are *still* people, and if you go about life feeling like some people are lower than you because of social status or other factors, do you even understand the grace of God at all? What separates you from them but chance? I urge you to look at people around you, different from you, who may have made mistakes you cannot fathom, and instead of shaking your head, think of the possibilities because that CAN be you!

Beneath social status, class, race, and other societal elements that differentiate us; we're all just sick people who need Jesus.

Anyways, come with me to **1 Samuel 9:6;** who recommended that Saul go to Samuel to get information on his missing donkeys and he ends up getting anointed as Israel's king? A servant, an 'ordinary' person. A servant also recommended David to the employ of Saul (**1 Samuel 16:18**); another servant recommended that Naaman go see the man of God to get healed of his leprosy (**2 Kings 5:2-4**).

In fact, throughout the Bible, we see not just servants, but ordinary, lowly people act out the will of God in different ways. We are all equal in the sight of God, He has no favourites! (**Romans 2:11**). They are even more special as God condemns anyone who mistreats them, likening it to mistreating Him (**Matthew 25:35-45**).

In the end, aren't we all SERVANTS of the Living God?

Let me tell you about an experience that I had recently regarding this.

13/03/2022

I have just arrived in Lagos from the East and the blazing heat is enough to make me enter the tyre of any plane going back to Enugu because…what is this heat? I know I'm a hot chic but I am learning work[12] from this Lagos heat, please. Anyways, I book a Bolt and make my way into the park where the driver is parked, only for him to tell me that the ride has to be offline.

I shake my head in that 'oh-no-not-again Lagos' manner and ask him why he was accepting rides online if the payment would be offline. He laughs and I turn around and try to book another ride - visibly annoyed. After failing twice, it dawns on me that there is a sort of cooperation between the Bolt riders at the airport to overcharge passengers. It seems unanimous and unless I love stress, I would have to go with it.

Now indignant, I want to utter some terrible words about how their actions make no sense, but at this point, another driver walks up to us and asks what the matter is. After explaining to him, he replies in Igbo, and my sister, who is with me, responds in the same lingo. Suddenly, the ice is broken, and we begin

---

[12] Nigerian Pidgin phrase which loosely means that two subjects *can't be compared; **I am not as hot as the Lagos blaze**.*

to banter about how the whole matter was unfair, but this guy explains how they have to pay every time they come into the park, and every driver just has to do it or ends up not making a profit.

To cut this long story short, simply because of how we do not speak rudely (even though I really wanted to, save for my sister), the driver reduces the price, which is about 4x the online price, and we get a move on. At one point, I start to joke with the driver, who is really dark and has a number of tribal marks on both sides of his face, about how he deceived me and how I did not like it. He quickly retorts that an old 'baba'[13], like him 'no fit deceive young girl like me[14].' His accent is very funny and he even starts to dance with the luggage he has picked up. The whole scene ends well.

Do you know? That interacting with people lower than your perceived class opens your eyes to things that you may have been blind to? I recently started being intentional about talking with conductors and drivers (the not-so-crazy ones, please) and it shocks me what I find sometimes. The sad truth is that these ones are used to being talked down on a lot, so you can imagine how their faces brighten up when they are greeted in that normal way, as it should be. We

---

[13] elderly man

[14] cannot deceive a young lady like me

must normalise treating people equally and this is reflected in how we communicate with them.

Abraham entertained strangers who were later revealed to be angels and from there, he got the chance to plead Lot's case and eventually save his life (**Genesis 18**). You may argue that Abraham had discernment to perceive their heavenly status but you do not need discernment to honour or help strangers. Good behaviour is your plug (**Hebrews 13:2**).

What is my point? There is an art to communication and you must know this as a child of God.

Ephesians 4:29 (KJV) implores us in this manner:

'Let no corrupt communication proceed out of your mouth, but that which is good to the use of edifying, that it may minister grace unto the hearers.'

I love how the message translation puts it:

'Watch the way you talk. Let nothing foul or dirty come out of your mouth. Say only what helps, each word a gift.'

Are your words gifts? Are you the type that will talk without caution under the umbrella of '*I am just trying to be honest?*' Then you are the fool in **Proverbs 18:2 (ESV)** that:

'takes no pleasure in understanding, but only in expressing his opinion.'

Amanda always says, '*Speak to people like you will be preaching to them in the next second.*' Imagine speaking rudely to a person and having to preach to them in the next minute; you would be labelled a hypocrite; which, in all honesty, you would be. So maybe you are right to react if you are provoked and they are wrong, but will it matter in God's grand scheme of things?

Another aspect of communication is the physical. I have met people who felt that because English is not their mother tongue, they were under no obligation to master it. I have no problem with accents; I believe they are cute, but why would you intentionally murder a language because you cannot speak it properly and refuse to learn? Brush up! It does not speak well of you, and it can potentially embarrass you.

Major parts of communication deal with our interaction with other people which is why it is so important to get it right. The Bible tells us that we have not seen God but if we love man then His love is brought to full expression in us. We are to live peaceably with all men! **(1 John 4:12, NLT; Hebrews 12:14)**. Words are the major means through which our motives are perceived for *'out of the abundance of the heart, the mouth speaks.'* **(Matthew 12:34)**.

If your mouth is only pouring out leftovers from what is in your heart, then it means that your words are the tangible format of what is in your heart. To prevent miscommunication, which can be dangerous, you must learn to communicate properly. It is true that the heart of men is desperately wicked, but if God has given us a heart of flesh, our words should be gifts and we will not pour out good and evil from the same tongue **(Jeremiah 17:9, Ezekiel 36:26, Ephesians 4:29, James 3:8)**.

From working with and leading a team at work, I know that people interpret messages differently based on where they are, mentally.

The art of communication involves seeking to know where a person is at a particular moment and tailoring your message, accordingly. Consider Abigail, Nabal's wife, and how she approached King David when he was angry at her husband (**1 Samuel 25**). That is wisdom!

At work, I always try to put myself second and ask the right questions to gauge their mental position before making demands. That a person is your subordinate does not warrant that you speak to them disparagingly. In fact, under no circumstance should you speak to ANYBODY in a manner that does not boast of love. This in no way means that insubordination or complacency should be tolerated; it should always be handled with wisdom. You can be stern and still be kind.

However, it is not just words like I have said before: everything you do communicates, which is why you must be conscious to pass across a message of the love of God. Do you walk into a room like you are trying to hide? Do you appear timid? Are you always trying to disappear? Do you let anger accumulate instead of resolving the issue early on? The Spirit of God gives sound mind; it is yours for the taking. Ask for it. From food, your physical appearance, attitude to work and everything in between - they all add up for the Kingdom of God.

•••

Since we are talking about communication here, I deem it necessary to talk about associations and relationships. You have heard before that *'birds of the same feathers flock together.'* The kind of company you keep does wonders for your devotional life and for helping spur you on to good works, including evangelism. Community and fellowship with the saints are God's idea and will always be.

Hebrews 10:25 (NLT)

'And let us not neglect our meeting together, as some people do, but encourage one another, especially now that the day of his return is drawing near.'

It is okay to pull yourself apart from people who no longer share the same faith with you. It may be hard, but it is necessary because you cannot be unevenly yoked with unbelievers (**2 Corinthians 6:14**). Say what you may but ungodly associations will drain your faith and make you struggle unnecessarily in your Walk of Faith.

It communicates a message of dishonesty if you keep friends who have you acting one way when you are with them and a different way when you are not. To this end, a cheat code for communication is this - *let the means and end be the love of God.*

Action point

Filter your communication. Be aware of everything that goes on around you. This takes practice and an unwillingness to neglect any aspect of your life, no matter how small. Everything connects, believe me. Keep **Ephesians 4:29** close to your heart. There is an art to communication; when communicating, ask yourself three questions:

1. How will the person I am talking to interpret this message based on what they are going through or where they are right now?
2. How do I make sure that my message is not misinterpreted?
3. What feedback will help me know that my message was communicated how I wanted it to be?

Keep the magic words close by, too: 'sorry,' 'please' and 'excuse me,' still work. God helping you, your communication with people will have them seeking after that wisdom, and you will have that chance to bring them to Him. When you do talk about Him, people will listen.

Journal prompt:

Take a moment to digest all that you have just read. What comes to your mind? Are there areas that need improvement? Is it something you have already started working on?

Proverbs 15:23 (NLT) -

'Everyone enjoys a fitting reply; it is wonderful to say the right thing at the right time!'

Confession: I declare that evil corruption will not proceed from my mouth but that my words will bless the hearers. My words heal, make right and impart the wisdom of God to everyone who hears, and their souls will be open to receive the light of God's Word through me—in Jesus' Name. Amen.

Are there areas that need improvement in your communication? What changes can you make to do better? Write out your starting steps.

7

Self-Awareness and Evangelism

Romans 12:3 (NLT) - *'Because of the privilege and author-ity God has given me, I give each of you this warning: Don't think you are better than you really are. Be honest in your evalu-ation of yourselves, measuring yourselves by the faith God has given us.'*

'Man, know thyself.'

- Socrates.

Self-awareness is the experience of your personality and indi-viduality. It is the ability to focus on *you*, and know how 'you' work. Self-awareness means you can objectively evaluate your thoughts, actions and behaviours; deduce what parts do not align with your values, and interpret the perceptions of other people about you.

Self-awareness is knowing what matters to you, and what you stand for. It is a deep knowledge of *who you are* beyond the name your parents bestowed upon you - for reasons best known to them - which you had no influence over.

The average person lies to themselves, not intentionally, but by refusing to hold themselves up to the sun and be courageous enough to see what the light reveals. Simply put, they would rather lie to themselves than face the truth. Is this you?

It was me. Sometimes, it is still me, but it's less these days than before. Let me tell you what changed that for me.

An honest friend

This time around, it was no revelation or tears from my sleep but this truth changed my whole life. My friend, we'll call him Eziokwu[15]; I have known him for years, but when the COVID pandemic happened, it gave me more time than I could manage and this got us reconnected.

One thing that stood out was his honesty in most situations - I say most because, you know... He was honest to a fault, and he made sure that it rubbed off on me. How? He always asked me the right questions and told me beforehand that '*I don't know*' was not an option.

It was hard. Hard. It led to many quarrels between Eziokwu and me. Sometimes, I felt he was just being spiteful and trying to provoke me for no reason. Soon enough, I grew to realise that honesty is the best policy and that the first lab rat in your life should be you.

---

[15] this Name/word means 'truth' in the Igbo Language

Often, Eziokwu would ask me a question, and for several reasons, I would say I did not know. That was a half-truth; that I did not know was a choice because I had failed to examine myself and pick out the truth. Telling the truth after years of self-deceit is a path that gets worse before it gets better but the best time to start is 10 years ago...or now.

Trying to be as honest as possible made me realise that:

- There were questions I had never asked myself
- There were questions that I avoided because they were hard to answer
- There were answers I did not want to know because I got comfortable lying to myself

The more Eziokwu prodded and prodded, I started to feel like a stranger in my own body. Walls came down, and truth went up. It made me a much better person because I began to know myself better with the Spirit of truth in me.

You have heard that you can lie to anybody but not to yourself. It is not true; you can lie to yourself. But guess who gets hurt the most? You.

Philippians 4:8 (NLT) says:

'And now, dear brothers and sisters, one final thing. Fix your thoughts on what is true, and honourable, and right, and pure, and lovely, and admirable. Think about things that are excellent and worthy of praise.'

Fix your eyes on what is true. The truth will consecrate every-thing else that you do. Remember that the Holy Spirit is the Spirit of truth; if He is in you, it must show. In the introduction of this book, I told you about how I felt like a failure because people were not very responsive to my evangelism; it took self-awareness to realise that it would take more than jamming Bible verses in their heads to open their hearts to God.

It took self-awareness for me to realise that people are at differ-ent points in their walk with God, and I must be responsive to that. It took self-awareness to be more compassionate toward unbeliev-ers because I used to be in that position and I knew how 'forceful' preachers had made me spite the religion even more.

I say this because to be a good judge of people's journeys and where they are; whether they are open to receiving the Word of God—you must be good at observing but this should begin with observing yourself.

Matthew 7:3 (NLT) speaks to the man that is not self-aware:

'And why worry about a speck in your friend's eye when you have a log in your own?'

Fix your thoughts on what is true because the opposite can be the case, as it is with people a lot of times. A person who is not self-aware is not fixed upon truth, they become blind to their faults, and this goes against the very tenets of Christianity that advocates for mercy. When we judge another person, we often forget that we are guilty of the same sins which God has shown us mercy for. In **Matthew 6:12**, Jesus teaches us to pray: *Forgive us our trespasses, as we forgive those who trespass against us...*

Jesus was very self-aware; we see throughout His life how He evaluated situations and knew what actions to take and when to take them. The very Word of God is described as a double-edged sword designed to expose 'our innermost thoughts and desires.' (**Hebrews 4:12**). That is Jesus!

Being aware of the things I did and telling myself the truth made me uncover many truths about myself, my errors that needed corrections and deficiencies that needed fixing. I am naturally not a confrontational person, so I would rarely raise my voice or even utter a sound if I am in an argument with another person.

Why? I discovered it's partially because I grew up writing and depended so greatly on this skill to think and untangle my thoughts rather than speak. Just wait for me after a quarrel, and I will certainly send you an expository epistle detailing your *mess-up*[16]! While this helped me not escalate tense situations, the flip side was that in situations where I did need to speak, I would keep quiet. I am learning now to discern when to speak and when not to.

Something happened to me during a visit with my friend, Faith, to one of her friends' places. Now, Faith was a girl I had known since I was a teenager, so she knew me pretty well - she knew how taciturn I usually was around new people. Her friend was not just a new person, though; she was also the epitome of a kind of character and

---

[16] Nigerian Pidgin expression for faults

lifestyle that I usually frowned at. I knew this by her hairstyle and how she was dressed. However, this was not the case on this day - I interacted with her like I would any other person. This was a HUGE deal for me! Spending time with God helped me see people through His eyes, not mine, log and all. We all need God. All of us. **When you meet people, the first value you should have for them is the value of their souls**, like God does.

Are your responses to situations mostly emotional? Are you fond of hiding behind the phrase, *'that's just how I am?'* Do you know the truth within you when asked a question but prefer to lie habitually because you do not know how to properly communicate the right answers or you just don't want to go down that lane? Then you are not self-aware. We cannot always get everything right. Sometimes, life happens, and you make a mistake; your response in such situations is key.

Do you know yourself? Here is how you can start being self-aware:

1. **Know your temperament:** I remember when Tim LaHaye's *Why You Act The Way You Do* was trending back in secondary school, and everyone wanted to be a Choleric. If this was you, how true is that now? Knowing your temperament is a good place to start being self-aware; do not be so strict or linear as you go about this. I have discovered that every person has a bit of each personality type but just in higher or lower ratios.

   I know myself enough to know that if I stay home too long, it affects me. Also, I know my strict routine-ish nature can have a counter effect, so sometimes I turn things upside down and freestyle. If anything, it's a reminder of why my routine works or is necessary. I know that when I am sad, I want to wallow, so I pick sad music over Spirit-filled ones that can give me a solution and uplift me. I know that if I start to sleep too much, I have a problem I am running from. I know that sometimes even if I feel like the world is ending now if I sleep and wake up, the world will start again. I know that when I turn to poetry over prose, it's a kind of therapy for when I am going through things I cannot properly express immediately. I know.

How well do you know yourself? Are you mature enough to be honest with yourself and make the necessary changes? Start being honest with who you are; your feelings, reactions and triggers, and the truth will find its home in you.

2. **Notice patterns:** What happened yesterday that has happened today? Go beyond noticing that each time you eat, you want to sleep. Notice patterns with yourself, your behaviours around different sets of people and environments; this will open your eyes to patterns in the things and people around you too. Besides, noticing patterns is the first step to correcting wrong ones.

3. **Set up reminders:** One thing that regularly plagues humans and Christians is forgetfulness. This is why it is important to set up mechanisms for when we do forget. Ebenezer was a stone set up to remind the Israelites of

God's help (**1 Samuel 7:12**). I tend to wallow in depressing moods, so I wrote somewhere (within my range of vision) that *'Choose not to wallow.'* This simple act has tremendously helped me. If you have a habit that you want to change, don't try to avoid it or pretend *'it's not that bad,'* take steps to solve it.

4. **Know your selling and not-selling points:** What part of you attracts people to you the most? You should know. You should play that up. If you meet me today, you will know that I am a writer; I not only write but talk like a writer - don't ask me how writers talk. Know the effect you have on others too; what is the first impression you often give out? Does it need to be corrected? God is the main character in your life, but after Him, it is you. Like I once said to my friend, anybody can tell you that you are not *'fine'* or *'all that'* but not you. To yourself, you must be IT. This does not mean that you are oblivious to your faults, it means that you are working on them, and in the meantime, nobody who is not a cheerleader has to have backstage passes to that *work in progress.*

5. **Learn to negotiate with yourself:** This is an integral part of self-awareness—talking to yourself. Talk to yourself and come to conclusions; you can do it in front of a mirror. Ask yourself why you picked certain actions over others or chose not to do something. If the *'why'* proves difficult, start by asking *'what'*: what triggered this? What were the dynamics? In everything, realise

that *'I don't know'* is not an answer. If you prefer, you can journal. In fact, self-negotiation is not complete without the art of writing. You should know how to write down your thoughts to better process and visualise them.

The art of self-negotiation is crucial, especially when you set goals. For example, you said you would finish the book of Romans in one week, and you did not. Why? Was it too long? Too tasking? Did understanding become more important than meeting the goal of finishing? These will give you feedback on how to make better negotiations so you set goals that you can attain next time. Also, it is easier to have a conversation with others after you have had it with yourself. You may have experienced people who always seem like they have a speech at the tip of their tongue - trust me, it is not without practice.

Self-negotiation is also how you start being truthful with yourself. Maybe you uttered a silent *'that's not me'* when you read earlier that most people lie to themselves but that response was just another lie which proves my hypothesis. Remember that time you wanted to say no but you ended up saying yes then tried to convince yourself that you wanted to say yes? That's lying to yourself. Most people also make a habit out of it until they do not even know the difference between a lie and a truth.

I'm no psychologist but if you make it a habit of lying to yourself, lying to people will become very easy for you. And it won't be intentional, it's just that you cannot hide such a well developed skill that you have consistently practised by always lying to yourself. It will show.

So, negotiate with yourself. Tell yourself the truth as much as you can. If you notice that you are hesitant to admit anything to yourself, that is a sign that you need to have some time off with yourself to figure 'you' out.

6. **Ask people around you:** Ask people you know to be truthful around you for their opinions on certain things about you; it helps to broaden the picture you have of yourself so you are not so narrow-minded. But always remember that what people tell you is also filtered by their own experiences and other factors that affect them, so you must be able to discern their answers by comparing several other answers from different people that you trust.

7. **Discern your feelings:** Yes, feelings are fickle. Yes, feelings change. But self-awareness demands that you know why. It may be as simple as food or as complicated as love, but you must know why you feel the way you do.

Cultivate the habit of pausing to reflect as often as you can, this will help you ask yourself necessary questions which will aid you in discerning your feelings. For example, if you suddenly find yourself annoyed at everything and everyone around you, you may be feeling quick-tempered because you've not had proper sleep; not necessarily because of any immediate cause. Pay attention to how you feel so that you can easily attribute certain feelings to certain causes. This will help you to respond to situations instead of reacting. It will also help you communicate effectively even when you are not *in the mood* or you are about to be impulsive or spiteful (this is where conflict resolution skills come in).

8. **See yourself in the mistakes of others:** One thing that is present in every human being is the occurrence of Tendencies. I once argued with a friend about jungle justice and how it was not that these people were not human, but they were just subject to the right (or wrong) conditions to trigger that savagery in them. If you have read *Lord of the Flies*[17], you will see the same pattern in little, well-brought-up English boys who were subject to the right conditions - a desolate land and no adult supervision - to become savages who carried sticks and tried to kill each other. The nature of sin makes this very possible.

When people make mistakes, do not frown at them. Introspect on how that could have been you. When you're confronted with the errors of others, can you see yours too? That's humbling. I once got very provoked at a co-worker who I felt was intentionally slacking on her tasks, but upon closer inspection, I was faced with the reality of how I had experienced a similar situation, and this gave me a better perspective to solve the issue.

---

[17] The 1954 novel by the Nobel Prize-winning British author William Golding

Self-awareness unlocks deep empathy, which we need to arm ourselves with as preachers of this Gospel. You must be self-aware so you don't focus so much on the log in your brother's eye. In fact, being self-aware means that you'll be too busy removing the speck in your eyes (because there is a lot of work that you need to do on yourself) to notice and begin to point out the flaws in another person. Also, it is when your eyes are free of specks that you can see clearly enough to remove the log in someone else' eyes.

Matthew 9:36 (NLT) tells us of Jesus' deep compassion for Israel:

'When he saw the crowds, he had compassion on them because they were confused and helpless, like sheep without a shepherd.'

You can be moved like this when you are self-aware enough to know that the world deserves the same mercy Christ has shown you. Instead of gossiping about a person's problems, you will be moved to pray for them. The Holy Spirit makes this possible!

I love the book *'Screwtape Letters'* by C.S Lewis. A particular place that stood out for me was the assertion that one of the most powerful tools of the devil is that the Christian man is kept as not-self-aware as possible. This blinds him to his faults while opening his eyes to the faults of others. For example, the subject hated how his mother sounded when she nagged but was blind to the fact that it was exactly how he sounded.

This describes a LOT of people. It might sound cliche but it remains true that when you point an accusing finger, four others are pointed back at you. Do you realise how silly you sound whenever you point out the faults of others in a haughty manner? Like it's something you'd never do? Like it's something beneath you? Take a closer look, you might just be conveniently blind to your faults. The next time you are triggered to complain about someone in that *holier-than-thou*[18] manner, turn on your Voice Memo and record your voice as you lay your accusations. You sound so silly. Yes, you.

Does this mean that you should let the faults of others slide? No. It means that you should treat others how you want to be treated. Love is key. Correct people with love and compassion. Pray for them first. If you still feel like complaining or gossiping about them afterward, you will need to pray some more. Pray until that desire flees.

'Confess your faults one to another ...' - James 5:16

Even in the presence of God, you must know yourself. Sometimes I get to church feeling blue, and it shifts my mood. I become irritable. When I notice this, I quickly pray to God. Otherwise, I would mess up my whole day for very fickle reasons.

Let the truth reside in your heart. It will make all the difference. With Spirit-led and intentionally developed self-awareness, you can

---

[18] self-righteous

truly know yourself, you won't follow the crowd or think something is wrong with you because something did not happen to you. You won't compare your path with others because you'll know that where you are in your walk with God is exactly where you're supposed to be and that everyone is on a different journey or path based on God's will for them. You will know all your '*whys,*' and you will be right. You will discern things from multiple perspectives. You will not be triggered to react; you will respond, instead. You will build better relationships. You will understand yourself, and this will lead to a better understanding of others. You will be free from assumptions. You will better regulate your emotions.

In the words of Charles Munger:

'Knowing what you don't know is more useful than being brilliant.'

I believe one word sums up the importance of being self-aware - humility. Self-awareness builds humility, which means that you are open to learning; this is essential as Jesus calls us to 'learn of Him,' the most GENTLE and HUMBLE at heart **(Matthew 11:29).**

I mentioned earlier in this book how I was often tempted to act in a way my family was used to before I got saved. This was not something I was initially aware of until the Holy Spirit brought it to my attention, and we took out time to examine why. The humility to be able to listen to God and take corrections when He points out your flaws is a direction that being self-aware will point you to and you will thank yourself for it.

Now, about this situation that I described with my family, I got to know that such a situation often happens with people you are too familiar with. You feel such an urge to blend in or be who they knew you to be. The result of this is that you may end up feeling like they're strangers and either want to stay away from them or act in a way they are used to—which is no longer how you are. None of these options will help! The way out of this is to hold on tight to the knowledge of what is true, one of which is that God loves them as much as He loves you and you can partner with Him for their salvation - that is - if they are not already saved. If they are already saved, it helps to remember that they are a part of the body of Christ, who have the Holy Spirit, and you must fellowship with them, too. Everything else will fall in place afterwards.

I believe the above scenario also relates to being a believer and still hanging out with unbelieving friends; people who may not understand your faith and may try to drag you back to your former way of life, intentionally or otherwise **(1 Peter 4:4)**. My advice on this one is RUN. The devil often shifts convictions gradually; the desire to sin is rarely outright—it begins with such compromise in the quality of your associations like this.

It is just like when people ask if alcohol is a sin or not, it is not a sin, just like hanging out with your unbelieving friends is not a sin. However, it can be a prompt to sin. It is something that can lead to sin. For example, alcohol in itself is not harmful, it is an ingredient in food and even skin products; however, when taken too much, it makes people lose their grip on reality and give away their self-control. This makes it a prompt to sin and presents a reason why it should be abstained from

The Bible is super clear on this:

1 Thessalonians 5:21-22 (KJV)

21 'Prove all things; hold fast that which is good.

22 Abstain from all appearance of evil.'

Therefore, if you happen to be in a situation that seems like it may trigger a wrong act, it is wise to flee. If you are often in the company of people who are not Christians, you are more likely to sin. Therefore, give the devil no chance or foothold in your life. Remember, **1 Corinthians 6:12 (MSG)** says, **'Just because something is technically legal doesn't mean that it's spiritually appropriate. If I went around doing whatever I thought I could get by with, I'd be a slave to my whims.'**

Above all, be God-aware, pay attention to His workings and commands, and let that pervade and influence every other aspect of your self-awareness journey. To know yourself truly is to first know God in whose image you were made. It is only when you know Him, that you can begin to make Him known.

Like Socrates said, 'Man know thyself.' If I could make a little edit, the saying would go this way instead; 'Man, *know thy God first and then you will know yourself.'*

Action point

Master self-awareness. Start in the presence of the Lord where it is easiest because He already knows all, so you have no need to hide a thing. Be honest with God. He always understands even when you do not. He will uncover your heart's truth because you cannot know yourself without God. The Word - in **Jeremiah 17:9** - says that the *heart of men is deceitful*; you cannot afford to trust such a heart without Christ in it.

Every disconnect - I have shone a light on in previous chapters - connects to self-awareness. Be aware but not overly conscious that you begin to prioritise the thoughts of others about you over God's. Be mindful. When trying to practise self-awareness: focus on one aspect of your life or habits at a time so you can know as much as possible about the factors that affect it and it does not overwhelm you. Eventually, self-awareness in one aspect of your life will impact every other aspect.

Most importantly, confess. Affirm God's Word over your life. When you have been honest with yourself, filter your actions and words through His Words and declare who you want to be! You will grow into that every day as you learn from your mistakes and improve.

Self-awareness holds facts supreme, just like being God-aware holds the facts, based on the knowledge of God, supreme. This helps you to be always conscious of the presence of God, no matter your feelings. It helps you remain devoted to God and fulfil the desires of the Spirit by the Spirit whether you 'feel' like it or not.

May God help us all.

Journal prompt:

Take a minute to flip through the start of this chapter back to the end. How do you feel? Now is a good time to head to your Light journal and detail all the ways you may have fallen short when it comes to self-awareness plus how you can improve. Do take cues from the 8 tips provided to get better at self-awareness too.

Romans 12:3 (NLT) -

'Because of the privilege and authority God has given me, I give each of you this warning: Don't think you are better than you really are. Be honest in your evaluation of yourselves, measuring yourselves by the faith God has given us.'

Confession: I declare that I am searched by the Spirit and made aware of everything that makes me, me: my flaws, my traumas, and my uniqueness even as I am healed from every negative behaviour. Above all, I am God-aware, and this affects how I treat myself and others, geared towards the ultimate goal of spreading the Gospel—in Jesus' Name. Amen.

Are there areas that need improvement in how you treat yourself or others? What changes can you make to do better? Write out your starting steps using the 8 tips provided as a guide.

8

Money and Evangelism

E cclesiastes 10:19 (KJV) - *'A feast is made for laughter, and wine maketh merry: but money answereth all things.'*

09/09/2021

It is a sunny day, very sunny. I keep wiping the sweat from my brows with the back of my hand. My I-just-got-back[19] - someone who just returned from overseas - friend is beside me; we have just left a park at Alausa. We are finding it difficult getting a ride so we have to walk a bit as the area is quite enclosed. Fun fact: I initially got us walking in the wrong direction (because I was sure I knew the route) when I could have just used my map and saved us a load of stress. Story for another day. Or not.

---

[19] Someone who just returned from overseas

Anyways, we are talking about money, specifically how the richest people in the world came about their wealth and how none of it seems to be legitimate or purely legal. This, we suggested, seemed to be why many Christians are on extreme ends of either poverty or prosperity Gospel. Here, it is easy to see the disconnect.

The next statement I utter makes me cringe every time I recall it. I say, rather boldly I must add, 'That kind of money is just ungodly.' My friend never lets me hear the last of it to this day.

Do you have this notion that Christians should not have so much money? It is not unfounded. Mine came from a strong deduction formed by accumulated opinions of people and society that stemmed from never or rarely ever seeing Christians - asides from Pastors - be that wealthy. And when Pastors are wealthy, the society I come from tags it as a problem; why should a pastor be *that* rich? He must be doing something wrong.

There is a long line of arguments concerning this, I will not go down that road. However, I do not think money is ungodly anymore. Here is why:

The world we live in now and even the world in Solomon's time understood one principle; that money answereth all things. Right? Maybe, but not in the way you interpreted the popular scripture. A deeper look at the context of that scripture reveals its simple meaning:

Ecclesiastes 10:19 (Good News):

"Feasting makes you happy, and wine cheers you up, but you can't have either without money."

Money may be the answer to everything material but it does NOT answer *everything*; this is a fact. Notwithstanding, it does not mean it is ungodly because it does have great utility. For Christians, one principle stands above all the others, and that is what we can see in **Matthew 6:33** -

'Seek the kingdom first, and all other things shall be added.'

I need you to see money as a *means to an end and not the end*. Things go wrong when you chase money. If you chase money, you will always want more. It will be an end, and it will consequently be your end. Remember the parable of the rich fool? His misplaced trust in his material possessions was his end **(Luke 12:16-21).**

Consider **Proverbs 23:4-5 (NLT),** which says:

'Don't wear yourself out trying to get rich. Be wise enough to know when to quit. In the blink of an eye wealth disappears, for it will sprout wings and fly away like an eagle.'

Money will come. Money will go. It is fleeting. If God gives you all that money you think you need right now, can you handle it? And if you can, what is the guarantee that you will not lose it tomorrow?

If you happened to be in an earthquake, you'd look to find the most stable structure above ground level to keep from being swallowed. In the same way, it is a wise investment to hold on to the most constant element in life that you can find. That constant is God. **Matthew 13:44** tells the inspiring story of a man who found a treasure and sold all he had to buy the field in which the treasure lay - such is the kingdom of God! The kingdom of God is the greatest investment any man can make, with huge returns on investment— this is why we must seek it first.

Take this example of the golden goose: if you had to choose between the goose that lays golden eggs and all the eggs she laid for a year, what would be your selection? You would go for the goose because that is the source! Yet, many of us choose money over God; we choose the eggs and not the goose. Is it not wiser to choose God who is the source of everything—money inclusive?

I repeat, money is not ungodly; however, its utility can be. As a Christian, money becomes a means to an end. It is a tool to fund the Gospel and set up structures that will favour and empower Christians to further push the agenda of the Kingdom. Your money can make people receptive to you in ways that the Gospel may not immediately make them.

Nevertheless, it is still not a reason to chase money. No. You chase God fervently and watch Him provide all you need for your ministry. If you doubt this provision, then you need to go back to the Bible to remind yourself of who God is.

•••

Another angle to money I would like to examine concerns all the previous chapters that I have examined a disconnect. From being intentional about food, your appearance, and even purpose, the thought may have flashed in your mind that to do these things will require some form of funding, right?

True.

However, more than that, it requires discipline to start from where you are. **If you cannot begin when you do not have everything you need, you will not start when you have everything you need.** Start from where you are. It will work out from there, because lack is first a state of mind. If I had been thinking about all the money I did not have, I would not have written this book. I had less than 1k in my bank account (don't laugh, I may have more faith than logic) when I started writing this book, and I had 1,300 when I decided to publish it (naira, not dollars). The truth is, your talent is even a form of capital, do not take it for granted.

Start from what God has put in your hands. God did not multiply the bread and few fishes in the hands of Jesus until He gave thanks and began to break them.

Mark 6:41 (NLT):

41 'Jesus took the five loaves and two fish, looked up toward heaven, and blessed them. Then, breaking the loaves into pieces, he kept giving the bread to the disciples so they could distribute it to the people. He also divided the fish for everyone to share.'

Whatever God has asked you to do, He will show you how to do it. **Trust the God who has called you to not only start but finish what He started.** You may think, alright, 'Maranatha is now aspiring to perspire,' but listen, everything I write here stems from experience: being in need, carrying lack on my head, having no idea where my next meal would come from, crying all night because of my zero account balance, having my heart break because my family had needs and I could do nothing to assist - God always came through for me. Now, like Paul, I know how to be content with whatever I have. For **'godliness with contentment is great gain.'** (1 Timothy 6:6, NIV).

Philippians 4:12-13 (NLT) goes:

'I know how to live on almost nothing or with everything. I have learned the secret of living in every situation, whether it is with a full stomach or empty, with plenty or little. For I can do everything through Christ, who gives me strength.'

Your smile should not change whether or not you have
shingbai[20] in your account. How can it be when your joy is found
primarily in God?

It will not happen in a day. It took a while to get a hold of this
truth and seal it in my heart. Do you know? At one point, I was con-
fident that God wanted me to be poor; nothing else could explain
this continuous lack I was experiencing in my life.

That day, the Holy Spirit urged me to do something that has
now become a habit whenever I am getting confused or unsure
about what God has said concerning me. How can the same God
who gives everything richly for my enjoyment (**1 Timothy 6:17**)
want me to be in constant lack? My God is not inconsistent that I
was sure of. That day, I went to Google and researched every Scripture that related to God's providential capacity, took screenshots,
and kept them all in a photo folder on my phone. Every time I
felt that way, I would go through all of them, and my mind would
reset. God's assurances were still very much valid and would continue to be.

Many times, when we falter in our walk, it can often be traced to
a weak knowledge of what God has said, as was my case. God spoke
severally to me during the periods when I prayed about my material lack, but I interpreted every one of His words to mean material blessings because that was what I was focused on. Thanks to
His patience, I finally got the much-needed mind shift, and I can
actively see God's blessings beyond the material. It is HUGE. Mind

---

[20] Nigerian pidgin expression for nothing

you. I have never been in lack since then. Everything I have needed, He has provided. And if He does not, then I do not need it.

The Scriptures present a very strong comparison between God and mammon.

Matthew 6:24 (NLT):

'No one can serve two masters. For you will hate one and love the other; you will be devoted to one and despise the other. You cannot serve God and be enslaved to money.'

This is a caution for all Christians to be wary of money. Nothing in this world provides security, albeit false, like money does. That security is one that only God should provide for us.

I am not a billionaire yet, but I can be with the things He has put in my hand. Still, that is not the goal; the kingdom is. Fix your eyes on the kingdom. Always.

Money management

Oh, you thought I would not come here? I have to. Money management is crucial for everyone who spends money - whether or not you make it is a gist for another day.

I'm putting this here because I want you to know that wise spending is demanded of you as a Christian. If we say all things are from God - money included - then we should be proper managers of God's resources.

It is not wise to spend money without care, no matter how much of it you make. Learn financial management skills, know how to split your money for different purposes based on priorities, and spend on the right things.

Ultimately, it's all for your good so that you will be financially independent - and not have to depend on other people - just like God wants you to be. Through wise spending, you will always have money when you need it.

1 Thessalonians 4:11-12 (NLT):

11 'Make it your goal to live a quiet life, minding your own business and working with your hands, just as we instructed you before.

12 Then people who are not believers will respect the way you live, and you will not need to depend on others.'

One money tip that has worked for me since I started to put it into practice - almost like magic - is this: *buy people, not things*. Don't fret…it is not human trafficking. You should invest your money in people, not things. Giving never goes out of style; you can use your money to make room for yourself in places. Do this wisely, not foolishly. Money is so valuable in our world today, and people attach such tremendous value to it: use this to your benefit. People who hold on so tightly to money soon discover their fatal error, and the consequences are often very costly.

Some people say money can buy happiness but It depends on what you describe as 'happiness'. I do believe that money can only buy the things that money can buy. If your money could buy anything that money should ordinarily not be able to buy, you should be very scared.

That being said, the beauty of money lies in its utility, not its possession. Use your money to put smiles on the faces of people. Use your money for the kingdom of God. Put your money where your mouth is: if you confess Jesus as your saviour and Christianity as your profession, then it is a requirement that you support Christian media, Christian programmes, Christian movements. Give to your local church, pay your tithe, support missionaries, give to your spiritual leaders, partner with your local churches to plant more churches for the spread of the Gospel, attend Gospel concerts. This is pleasing to God.

Action Point

Laser focus on God first. God first, not mammon. The money is for the kingdom, and it will show up when needed. Believe this: Even your talent is a form of capital, so do not take that for granted or let money hinder you from doing anything you want to because *when God moves, you must move.*

Manage, properly, the resources that God has given you. Above all, use your money to fund the Gospel, no matter how small you feel it is. It is necessary as a part of the body of Christ. Remember, the prevalence of the Gospel and the kingdom of God is the end; money is only a means.

May the Holy Spirit open your eyes to the light of His Word— in Jesus' Name. Amen.

Journal prompt:

Take a minute to reflect on all that you just read. Is anything nagging on your mind? Does anything stand out in your life concerning how you think about money? Are there any formerly held misconceptions that come to the top of your mind?

Ecclesiastes 10:19 (KJV) -

'A feast is made for laughter, and wine maketh merry: but money answereth all things.'

Confession: I confess that money, to me, is merely a tool for the dissemination of the Gospel. My money works for the things of God and makes way for the people and things of God. Above all, *my* money is not my money: I am, but a manager of God's resources, and I do this well by the strength of the Holy Spirit in me—in Jesus' Name. Amen.

Are there areas that need improvement in your spending? What wrong thoughts do you have about money? What changes can you make to do better? Write out your starting steps.

9

What Now? 10 Keys to Evangelism

Romans 15:20 (KJV) - *'Yea, so have I strived to preach the gospel, not where Christ was named, lest I should build upon another man's foundation.'*

From the previous chapters you have read, you may now think evangelism to be harder or simpler than you previously envisioned it to be. I aim for neither of those thoughts. Evangelism is making God known; more than shouting *'the kingdom of heaven is at hand,'* with the loudest voice you can muster, it must reflect in your everyday life, too.

Personal development is essential, more than ever, because you are saved; use it to your advantage. The secular world has got it right and so should you in order to use that influence for the kingdom of your Father. Imagine you always look good and healthy; you're well-mannered, knowledgeable and strategic; that - in itself - is influence and power. In fact, this is what makes up the resume of many influential people. Now, combine this with the Holy Spirit, you will be unstoppable.

Some people know this as 'lifestyle evangelism', where you start to preach the Gospel right from your appearance or demeanour. However, I like to see it as the beginning stage of evangelism because it often makes people welcome your presence even without knowing what you're about to say.

Every single day - and in everything you do - you must spread God and the Gospel. If anything, you should know now - at this point - that everything connects to God. You do not have to be a 'preacher' to share God; you only have to be a believer. How can you tell people *how God wants them to live* if you cannot live the way He wants you to live? What if you are the closest Christian your work-mates ever encounter?

I have taught you to live the Gospel. Still, this does not displace the good ol' preaching or evangelism as we know it. A combination of these will be a game-changer in your devotional life. **Living the Gospel does not replace preaching the Gospel - ONLY THE GOSPEL SAVES (Romans 1:16).** It is the knowledge of God that shines a light in the darkness found in the hearts of men.

Romans 10:13-15,17 (NLT):

13 'For "Everyone who calls on the name of the Lord will be saved.

14 But how can they call on him to save them unless they believe in him? And how can they believe in him if they have never heard about him? And how can they hear about him unless someone tells them?

15 And how will anyone go and tell them without being sent? That is why the Scriptures say, "How beautiful are the feet of messengers who bring good news!

17 So faith comes from hearing, that is, hearing the Good News about Christ.'

But guess what? It is much easier to preach the Gospel when you live it. A Christian does not live a life of contradictions between the Word and their lifestyle.

Letting your light shine so that men will see your works (**Matthew 5:16**) is so important. Your faith inspires your works. People may not know the Gospel, but they know you. They may not perceive God but they can see you. You must let your light draw people to you, then you - go ahead to - give them the Gospel that saves. You can attract people to the Gospel.

Every aspect of The Disconnect I have touched on affects the individual lives of Christians because these parts are often neglected, and it should not be so. You should not dim the light of God in your life. Let it shine. If you cannot take care of yourself and fully be 'YOU' by the Spirit, how will you take care of other people? Diligence in small matters first, remember. Love yourself first as God loves you, remember.

One Thing You Cannot Do In Heaven

The above is the title of a book by Mark Cahill that partially encouraged the 40 Days Project. One profound thing I took from the book was that you can never lose with evangelism. Three things happen when you evangelise:

1. Unbelievers accept Jesus
2. You plant a seed
3. You get rejected

All cases present a win for you; how? Even when you get rejected, you are in the good company of prophets - before you - who have been rejected for Christ. As a matter of fact, the Word calls you 'blessed.' How is that for a start?

In communication, the first step is exposure. You can surely scrap the rest of the steps involved in passing across a message if people are not exposed to a message in the first place. The point here is to reiterate that faith comes by hearing the Word of God, and you have the duty to preach that Word of God, so people are exposed to it.

How to evangelise:

It is not a checklist. Repeat after me, *'evangelism is not a checklist.'* I say this because it often seems so. *'Tell Brother Pius about Jesus, check. Tell Sister Janet about Jesus, check. If they say no, remove your bata*[21] *(slippers) and dust it off; take your peace with you.'* No, it's more than immediately writing people off if they refuse to listen to you.

Sometime this year, I watched a TV broadcast from a church about their plans to evangelise the world. The plan was this: if 1000 people or so should sign up and evangelise to a person every day for 100 days, they would be able to tell - do the maths - a certain number of people about Jesus.

I loved the practicality, down to the numbers but a part of me encountered a sort of sadness. Here is why: when I started my 40 Days Project to tell a person about Jesus every day in this same way, it flopped for several reasons:

1. On some days, I could barely tell myself about Jesus, let alone tell another person

2. I reduced the Gospel to only its verbal aspects, this meant that I only counted myself to have shared the Gospel with a person when I took out a part of the Bible and said it. If you have read this book up until this point, you know that such opportunities do not always arise. This is why we must learn to live the Bible, too.

3. Evangelising in this manner, one person per day, made me robotic for a reason. As long as I told a person about Jesus, that was okay, nothing further. I would check it off my list. No follow up, nothing.

---

[21] slippers or flip-flops

I hoped there would be a form of training or structure to prevent these 1000 from becoming robotic about the Gospel. The Word - filled with love - is practical and it is far from robotic.

To this end, my voyage into the very thing I was made for (evangelism) has taught me these 10 keys, which I am about to share with you. You are not allowed to skim through; let these keys be nestled within you as you prepare to carry and share Jesus wherever you go and through whatever you say or do.

Key 1: Offer value

If you examine the pattern of Jesus in the Bible as He gathered crowds to minister to, you will notice something very essential—He always offered something first. **Luke 6:19 (NIV)** offers profound insight: *'and the people all tried to touch him, because power was coming from him and healing them all.'*

Do you think the people gathered to listen to Jesus all came because they were primarily interested in the Gospel? That is untrue.

Jesus in **John 6:26 (NIV)**, says - seemingly dismally - **'Very truly I tell you, you are looking for me, not because you saw the signs I performed but because you ate the loaves and had your fill.'**

He knew. Nevertheless, He still offered that value because it is important: Some wanted healing, He gave **(Luke 6:19)**; others wanted bread, He gave **(John 6:1-14)**; even His disciples wanted to sit at His left and right - to be given some sort of prominence (**Mark 10:35-37**). Our dear Peter followed Jesus after He multiplied His fish; they had waited for a Messiah for so long and He finally showed up. Who wouldn't follow such a man who was supposed to save them? (**Luke 5:1-11**). Nathaniel followed JESUS after JESUS gave him a word of knowledge (**John 1:45-51**) and lots more. Pay attention and you will notice this pattern.

We often think that people should jump at us when we preach the Gospel; if it was that simple, why did it take so long for you to be saved?

What is valuable to you (the Gospel) may not be valuable to unbelievers simply because they do not know its value, nor can they appreciate it. In a sharp contrast, you can make them see its value. This does not always happen at once, which is why you may have to offer value to them in terms of what is valuable to them; Jesus modelled this, giving healing or mercy to those who desired it.

People are going through a lot: some are hungry, sick, and depressed, and all of these constitute obstacles to their assimilation of the Gospel. They put these struggles first. It is selfish, but it is what it is. For example, I did not come to Yeshua seeking to be an evangelist. That was not even within my frame of desires. I came looking for peace and rest from a world that kept taking from me without giving me anything in return. I found that peace, but God opened my eyes to more. And here I am.

Everything I have drawn as a connection between its elements and evangelism is a form of value. From food to your appearance.

How? Through the Spirit's capacity, you should be living a full life that boasts of all these!

My friend, Eziokwu once said -

> *'You cannot make something shallow and use God as a cover.'*

Just because you are preaching the Gospel does not oblige anyone to listen to you. Even you, won't you be scared if everyone you told to follow you actually does so without you offering any form of value to them in return? Such a scenario reminds me of a character in a cartoon who thought he was going to be made a god by his people after being randomly discovered by them; only to realise they only wanted to sacrifice him (literally throw him into a volcano) for the betterment of their land. If you are not offering any value and people want you around, then something fishy is probably going on.

Offer value first, then you can have a level ground to trade on.

Key 2: Nurture the Ground

Matthew 13, the famed Parable of the Sower, is often cited as an anecdote to pass across the message of the constancy and potency of the Word vis-à-vis the ground on which it is planted, namely, the hearts of men. God's Word is always fruitful, but the hearts of men may either be fertile; which lets it grow, or they may be laced with weed which ensures that the Word is choked. While many feel this transfers the burden of belief to the listener of the Word, I see something else here for the preacher of the Word - NURTURE.

Matthew 13: 3-9 (NIV):

3 'Then he told them many things in parables, saying: "A farmer went out to sow his seed.

4 As he was scattering the seed, some fell along the path, and the birds came and ate it up.

5 Some fell on rocky places, where it did not have much soil. It sprang up quickly, because the soil was shallow.

6 But when the sun came up, the plants were scorched, and they withered because they had no root.

7 Other seed fell among thorns, which grew up and choked the plants.

8 Still other seed fell on good soil, where it produced a crop—a hundred, sixty or thirty times what was sown.

9 Whoever has ears, let them hear.'

Nurturing is what God did for you and me. It is how He has led you up until this point. Patiently. Step by step. While the ground can be infertile, can it not be nurtured? Yes, it can. Many people you may evangelise to are rarely at that point where they are willing to let go of it all and start to follow Jesus. Some want to, but do not know how to let go - like the rich young man who could not bear the thought of losing all his riches to follow Jesus (**Matthew 19:16-22**). For this man, we often feel that all hope is lost, but it is not. It may take a while, but he may eventually leave it behind and follow. You know the human nature; you are human. Many things led to the point where you finally accepted Christ. I grew up in a Christian family, and Sunday school made me think I knew who Jesus was; even though I did not, but that knowledge helped me in the process of knowing Jesus. My point? It takes time.

You must begin to see evangelism as an investment that requires time to mature because it is, and it does. Was God not patient with you till this day? Are we not to imitate Him as His children? **Ephesians 5:1** says so. **Matthew 13** lauds the fertile ground above all, but many things contribute(d) to the fertility of the soil - its environment, the weather, and more. In places where the soil is not so good, it can be made so. See evangelism in this way: the ground can be nurtured.

You will not nurture forever; that is a fact. You were not where you were yesterday, right? In the same way, though we enter as babes in Christ, eventually, we become able to eat strong meat as mature Christians. The same goes for the ones you will preach to **(1 Corinthians 3:1; Hebrews 5:14).**

I have written here on how - in some cases - I started by first offering to pray for the people I (had intentions of) preaching to. This opens their hearts to whatever you want to say; it softens them. That you can do something without being asked is valuable, it nurtures the ground, and even if you do not eventually lead that person to Christ, you have contributed to their journey just like many workers in God's vineyard contributed to yours. As one body, in Christ, we work together by building on the foundations of many before us just as many after us will build. **If a person hears about Christ from multiple sources, He is more and more predisposed to the message.**

Always ask yourself as you preach to people, *'where is this person, and where can I meet them?'* The right answer will get you on the right path to nurturing the soul of their heart. The Holy Spirit will always guide you to do the right things.

Key 3: Follow up

Apostle Paul's missionary journeys lay the foundation and relate the importance of follow-up in evangelism. If you have read the various letters he wrote, he captures the different problems that conflicted with the new knowledge of God in the lives of these new converts: from the Corinthians, who had spiritual gifts but had more chaos than order in its dispensation, to the Galatians who seemed to base their justification in Christ by their preconceived idea of sanctification and personal merit.

This is why follow-up is important. The Gospel of Christ is new and unwanted by the desires of the flesh. Therefore, there will always be opposition, worsened by a lack of Christian communion or fellowship. When you evangelise to a person, follow-up does four things:

1. It lets them know that they are not alone, because it can feel that way sometimes, especially if they have no friend who is (a) Christian. Thus, you provide godly company for them which is very important for their growth.

2. It shows that you are not just looking for converts to add to your evangelism portfolio but you are invested in the wellbeing of the new convert.

3. It presents an opportunity for the new convert to have a faith mentor or a person to ask questions because they will have many questions.

4. It lets you keep track of a convert's growth and offer vital help along the way. The consistency also helps the new convert to integrate properly into this new way of living. See what **Colossians 4:12 (KJV)** says:

12 'Epaphras, who is one of you, a servant of Christ, saluteth you, always labouring fervently for you in prayers, that ye may stand perfect and complete in all the will of God.'

As Epaphras laboured in prayers for the Colossian Christians, so must you pray fervently for those you preach to that they come into the true knowledge of God. The way of the flesh that they walked in wars against their new knowledge of the Spirit. Interceding in this way, too, is an important element of follow-up.

Follow-up, in my opinion, is simply not negotiable except in situations where it is not possible. The Holy Spirit did not just convict you of unbelief when you were a sinner. He stayed. The equivalent of that for us evangelists (that is, every believer) is follow-up.

Key 4: Do not set unrealistic goals

It's easy to say you want to evangelise to a person, daily, but I do not see how possible that is, especially if you have other work that occupies your time. Wisdom is profitable. You cannot abandon your paid job, for instance, because you want to go out and preach; that contradicts the Gospel that beseeches the body of Christ to work like we're working for God. That being said, all work is still for God.

You can flourish where you are and start talking to everyone who you have opportunity to meet about Christ. It may not be pre-planned, but you must take the opportunity when it comes. As time goes on, you can start to put up a structure for maybe a person or two per week and progress from there.

I have said before that evangelism is not a checklist where you tick off names of people that you're no longer responsible for because you have preached to them. Each person is an investment; treat them as such.

One thing about setting unrealistic goals is that it will drain you and leave you feeling like you are doing something wrong. You start to feel guilty because you could not reach it. God does not want that for you. While the numbers matter, remember that God is a personal God; reach out to the people you can and proceed from there as you grow.

Key 5: Start from the people you know

I know a prophet is often not accepted in his home, but that is no excuse. The least you can say is that you tried. In the first chapter of this book, I touched on how I felt the need to conform to the old image of me that my family used to have because it was more familiar. At one point, I didn't even want to pray with them; it felt so weird. I could barely reconcile my new faith with them, and the reason was that my first genuine and personal experience of Christ had come from without.

It took the Holy Spirit to let me know I had a role to play in my family. So, I began to pray earnestly for them and acted out in a manner representative of my faith. I learnt to apologise when I was wrong, do chores at home despite having a full job, and do many other things I would usually shrug off or be nonchalant towards. It made them realise I was changed, and they opened up more to the idea of genuine Godliness.

That being said, your family is important. You may come from a family where it is not so easy to preach or live out your faith, but I will encourage you to try. I'm rooting for you, keep trying, and the Spirit will keep helping you.

You will be guilty if you have never even tried to bring your family or close friends in on the Good News. If not them, then who?

Key 6: Always remember to Dwell

Mary and Martha **(Luke 10:38-42)** present a classic archetype of this principle: while Mary dwelt at the feet of Jesus, Martha worked in the kitchen to entertain her guest and make Him feel at home. While Mary did make the better choice, Christians cannot always be Mary; we have to be Martha, too, for there is work in His vineyard to be done.

Wisdom is profitable; do not get so carried away working for God that you forget to dwell in God. No one can hold on to God's will for long without returning to His presence for the reaffirmation of that will - it is simply impossible. It is through prayer that a remembrance of God's will is provoked and this gives you strength to keep going. How do you know your next steps? How do you know what to stop and what to continue? We often lack wisdom, an abundance of which we find at His feet.

James 1:5 (NIV)

'If any of you lacks wisdom, you should ask God, who gives generously to all without finding fault, and it will be given to you.'

I have found myself getting carried away many times; once by my followers' growth on Instagram, I began to post more of what I felt people liked (being trendy) than things that preached the Gospel. Another time, testimonies and lauding poured in, and I became tempted to take His glory for me. I found my correction and realignment at His feet. At one point, I entered auto-pilot mode where I felt

I knew all I needed to do, so I prayed less and worked more - thanks to Christian company, I got corrected.

Dwell. Dwell more than you work. Dwell, and you will see the effect in your work. Dwell, through prayer, fellowship with the saints, Bible study and more; you will see that things will move faster. Doors, meant for you, will open everywhere. God will let you in on His plans. You will know things before they happen. You will know what to do and when to do it. You will know what steps to take next. DWELL!

Key 7: Learn to answer (hard) questions

I once encountered a girl who had questions she thought nobody could answer, leading her to disbelief in God. When she asked me the question, I shook my head. Not only was this question relatively cheap, but it also made me aware that she was not looking for answers because if she was, she would have found them a long time ago. An ordinary Google search would have done the trick.

You will often meet such people who think they are not doing what they are supposed to because they do not have certain answers. While I'm sure there are multiple reasons for these, none hold water. Nevertheless, the only way you can uncover this unintentional self-deceit is to have the answers to these questions backed by Scriptural references in your pocket.

Questions like 'why good people die, and bad people live?' If incest was permitted in the Bible? if God permitted bloodshed and slavery? What is the sin that leads to death and the sin that doesn't? The answers are in front of you if you look for them. The problem is not the answers unless you're seeking to argue; if the Jews saw signs and wonders yet did not believe, nor would the correct answers make such people believe. The problem is that they do not have the Holy Spirit. They do not need to be convinced. They need to be convicted.

While these answers are not only important for them, as a Christian, you must know these answers as it builds and strengthens your faith. Aside from research and studying, a good way to have these answers is to have Godly discussions with Christians around you; you'd be surprised at how enlightening this can be.

To preach the Gospel, you must know the Gospel in and out. Study the Word extensively; just like you would an exam. If Jesus said in **Matthew 4:4** that man shall not live by bread alone but by every Word that proceeds from the mouth of God, then you must study the Word of God as much as you eat physical food. It's complementary!

In the same way you can plan to go to a restaurant to try out new or foreign dishes - or plan what you'll eat for lunch or dinner - how about you transfer that intentionality to your spiritual feeding too?! Have Bible study dates! Set aside time to do an in-depth study on different books of the Bible! Don't just read, STUDY! Use commentaries, read in multiple versions; KNOW THE WORD! The Word of God is food for your spirit, eat it in large portions and as many times as possible.

Here's a final note on answering hard questions: Never let your desire to be seen as 'smart' or 'knowledgeable' override God's desire that someone, through you, may come to the knowledge of Him. If you do not have the answers, seek them; don't guess or assume because you want to keep up a reputation as a *Bible Scholar*. What is most important is the Word of God, correctly dissected and interpreted, so that those seeking the truth may find it and become free (**John 8:32**).

Key 8: Preach what is most important

Preachers often throw a sort of bait in the form of the blessings people get by believing in God. While I do not misunderstand this, there is something more important that should be communicated during evangelism. That thing is SONSHIP.

The Gospel is that Jesus died and we receive life by His death; that our sins are washed away and forgotten so we are reconciled with our Father once more; that sin has no hold over us, neither do we have any obligation to it (**Romans 8:12**); that we take upon ourselves the responsibility of the Great Commission (**Matthew 28:19-20**) to bring this Good News to everyone around us; and that we are where He is, always. The Gospel is that who you were before - *no matter how terrible* - does not matter, because you become new (**2 Corinthians 5:17**) once you accept the sacrifice of Christ who chose to be crucified (**John 10:18**) to pay for your sins. The Gospel is the '...**power of God at work, saving everyone who believes...**' (**Romans 1:16, NLT**).

Reconciliation with our Father is the most important thing about salvation, and this must be said—not what they can get from God or what will happen in hellfire. I once came across a church that printed a whole banner in front of their church specifying the punishment for each sin in hellfire. For example, for wearing hair extensions or jewellery you could get flogged 10 strokes of *koboko*[22]. It was as laughable as it was misleading; and gullible people might (will) fall for it. Stop giving Satan free PR!

Preach what is most important, that through the sacrifice of Jesus we are reconciled to our Father in Heaven! We have eternity in us! We have the Holy Spirit! We have peace and joy everlasting! Hallelujah!

Key 9: Do not be afraid

Do not be scared because your fear can become tangible. A Scripture in Jeremiah always comes to mind when I think about this.

Jeremiah 1:7,17 (CSB) says:

7 'Then the Lord said to me: Do not say, "I am only a youth," for you will go to everyone I send you to and speak whatever I tell you.'

17 Now, get ready. Stand up and tell them everything that I command you. Do not be intimidated by them or I will cause you to cower before them.'

---

[22] cane or switch for flogging

Do not be afraid! If you have fear in your heart, you hinder God's work through you. Do you know WHO you represent? The Most High, whose perfect love casts out fear. How's that for reassurance?

Paul said to Timothy something you should keep close to your heart:

1 Timothy 4:12 (NLT):

12 'DON'T LET ANYONE THINK LESS OF YOU BECAUSE YOU ARE YOUNG. Be an example to all believers in what you say, in the way you live, in your love, your faith, and your purity.'

Another way to think about it is to imagine you had the secret to making everyone smile; would you not tell it to everybody you saw frowning on the road? You certainly would! Now go tell it on the mountain.

Key 10: The multiplier effect

Do you know what is the most beautiful thing about the Gospel? I call it 'THE MULTIPLIER EFFECT.' Whenever I share the Gospel, I think to myself, *'Maybe he's the next Billy Graham or Adeboye,'* because you never know! The person with whom you share the Gospel may be that person that ends up doing great and marvellous works for God.

Bonus Key: Invite them to church

The church is God's presence here on earth. How? Since God dwells within each Christian, it means that when we gather, we are an assembly of temples. This is how the church is God's tangible presence on earth. In a church, many elements interplay to make a person believe: the presence of God, which causes signs and wonders; the fellowship of the saints; the aura of love; edification from the pulpit; psalms from the heart, and so much more.

Often, there is so much you can say; why don't you invite them to church? The church I made up my mind to attend frequently in school was God's starting point with me that led to my salvation. I was in a church where I felt love and peace, and when I saw how fellow students interacted with each other, it became a place I always wanted to be in. My salvation became an eventuality, not a possibility.

Invite them to church. They will surely grow in a community. Fellowship with the saints is God's idea. The relationship we have with Him thrives in community.

•••

In an online meeting in 2021, I was asked a question that went like this: *If you're going to preach to people in an area who, for example, believe that women should not wear trousers but the preacher who is female wears trousers, what should she do?'*

For the Gospel, I am anything. If you have to wear skirts, by all means, do - as long as you are not sinning. Follow Apostle Paul's example here:

1 Corinthians 9:19-22 (KJV):

19 'For though I be free from all men, yet have I made myself servant unto all, that I might gain the more.

20 And unto the Jews I became as a Jew, that I might gain the Jews; to them that are under the law, as under the law, that I might gain them that are under the law;

21 To them that are without law, as without law, (being not without law to God, but under the law to Christ,) that I might gain them that are without law.

22 To the weak became I as weak that I might gain the weak: I am made all things to all men, that I might, by all means, save some.'

To whatever man, I am what he is if that will bring him to Christ. If you're going to preach in a rural area, for example, there is a certain way you might overdress that may turn some people off, so you should dress accordingly to ensure your 'freedom' does not hamper the birthing of another person's faith.

I believe Christians should learn to be inventive in evangelism; the way you teach affects how people perceive the Gospel. The Word is always effective but your teaching also has to be effective. For example, if you are going to preach in a rural area, *pidgin* English is going to help you more than *spri-spri*[23].

2 Timothy 2:24-25 (CSB) confirms this:

'The Lord's servant must not quarrel, but must be gentle to everyone, ABLE TO TEACH, and patient, instructing his opponents with gentleness. Perhaps God will grant them repentance leading them to the knowledge of the truth.'

In **Acts 17:22-34**, Apostle Paul brought forth an argument of logic to the men of Athens and found a way to connect their worship of an unknown God to the Scripture - that is ingenuity. Some people will never listen to you as long as you start your preaching from the Bible. They simply do not believe. What do you do then? Start from where they are willing to start from. In listening to them, you will surely find a loophole to inject the Gospel.

Even Christians can be weak in this regard. There are some Christians who pride some things over others, in the manner of eating or even dressing or worshipping on certain days to give God honour. In such cases, your job is not to judge anybody's actions as right or wrong - insofar as it's not a sin - but to adjust to them, pray and contribute to their Christian growth because one day, they will

---

[23] Queen's English or the accent traditionally regarded as standard for British English

become more mature and outgrow such things as they upgrade in the knowledge of the truth.

In fact, the very fact that a person chooses to do certain things or abstain from certain things for the purpose of consecration or because they believe God does not like them is beautiful and commendable. (Do study **Romans 14** for profound insight on this). I mean, John the Baptist comfortably wore an outfit that was uncommon during his time because it was required of Him for Ministry **(Mark 1:6)**.

If you happen to find yourself in a place that might not be so accepting of your faith, I say, blend in until you have to stand out. Daniel in the king's palace '**...purposed in his heart that he would not defile himself with the portion of the king's meat, nor with the wine which he drank: therefore he requested of the prince of the eunuchs that he might not defile himself.' (Daniel 1:8, KJV).** He accomplished this through the wisdom of God. It would have been easy for him to go along. After all, he was a captive in Babylon, and nobody would blame him. Still, he stood out in ways that mattered.

Consider the fire boys (Shedrach, Meshach and Abednego) who lived in a foreign palace and even took on Babylonian names. However, they stood out when it came to an issue on which they could not compromise; better the furnace than to deny their God. Better to be with God in the storm than without Him in the 'calm.'

Now you must know that when you share the Gospel, the reward may not be instantaneous; sometimes, I preach, and I feel like I've wasted my time, and other times the person expresses such gratitude that it makes me feel so good - I'm sure I've done something good. But both scenarios are not markers of if indeed, the Gospel has penetrated the heart. The ultimate proof is time. Time will tell the effectiveness of evangelism.

How can you then know? You cannot. It may show up in good works later but rarely at the moment. So do your part and leave the rest to God.

By 'do your part,' you must know that you must STUDY THE WORD and PRAY. Before, during, and after evangelism - as much as you can. Pray. The Holy Spirit is the ultimate evangelist. The funny thing about evangelism is that you might sound good in your ears and by your judgement, but the other person may understand nothing that you're saying. This is why you're not gunning for what you perceive is 'right' or 'sounds good' but what the Word says and what the Spirit puts in your heart for the other person's good.

A simple hack for evangelism then, is going with the Holy Spirit so He gives you insight on the perfect way to reach each person's heart. Even though this is no guarantee that they will accept the Word, it is your best bet. Jesus only needed to tell the Samaritan woman about her polyandric ministry for her to believe (**John 4:5-28**).

Pray. Pray that the hearts of the lost are open to receive God's light. Pray. Don't stop praying. Pray and intercede for the lost. Pray!

When you share your faith, you do it with meekness, as proposed in **1 Peter 3:15**. You don't become pushy; you cannot enforce your beliefs on another person simply because you are right. To the other person, you might just be another raving religious fanatic. It is so important that you start with prayer to simply join the work of the Holy Spirit in their lives. You do it with empathy, come down to where they are, and find ways to connect with them.

Practice makes perfect. The more you evangelise, the better you get at it. Asides from your personal evangelism, amplifying the voices of others in the faith is evangelism, too, and should be done with as much fervour. We are, after all, one body in Christ.

•••

I wish to emphasise an issue I find very rampant among Christians which is diluting or exaggerating the Gospel. They are both sides of the same coin. One sect rages that unbelievers will perish in the lake of fire, and the other seems to insist that God is so merciful that He overlooks justice - that God is okay with whatever you do as long as you come. Or the excessive focus on what God will *do* for you materially.

Remember that God is a God of love and justice, just as He is your friend and your Lord. Both sides balance each other. In the same vein, sin does have a penalty. You cannot preach in such a way that people fail to realise this. It breeds ignorance of the truth. If sin was not such a big deal, then why the magnitude of such a sacrifice as Jesus?

Isaiah 59:2 (NIV) says,

2 'But your iniquities have separated you from your God; your sins have hidden his face from you...'

God hates sin and for good reason, sin separates Him from His children.

2 Corinthians 5:11 (KJV) goes:

11 'Knowing therefore the terror of the Lord, we persuade men; but we are made manifest unto God; and I trust also are made manifest in your consciences.'

NLT will help you understand it better:

11 'Because we understand our fearful responsibility to the Lord, we work hard to persuade others. God knows we are sincere, and I hope you know this, too.'

To preach the Gospel is a fearful responsibility! This is the Word that saves men from eternal damnation, so we cannot afford to get it wrong. We must stop teaching lies; an exaggerated or diluted Gospel is no longer the Gospel of Christ. If you stray from the truth, no matter how little, then you lie. Say what is in the Bible, do not remove or add to it **(Proverbs 30:6)**.

Wisdom is profitable to direct. Neither of these ways works; bringing people to the kingdom of God either through fear or half-truths is not sustainable. You can see this play out in the lives of many Christians who were taught to only fear and not love God - it drove them far from Him. For these people who grew up listening to how God will *punish them* for this and that: it gets so hard to remove that kind of hindering mindset from their hearts.

What punishment? When God has declared us who believe 'free of sin', for His own sake?

Isaiah 43:25 (NIV):

'I, even I, am he who blots out your transgressions, for my own sake, and remembers your sins no more.'

Hebrews 4:16 (NIV);

'Let us then approach God's throne of grace with confidence, so that we may receive mercy and find grace to help us in our time of need.'

So, can we come boldly?

Some preachers feel that people cannot digest the truth of the Bible - of course, they can't! But better they say, **'this teaching is hard; who can understand it?'** (**John 6:60**) and become mature eventually by the Spirit than accept lies that agree with their seared conscience. You are not doing anybody any good when you dilute the Gospel - you are only encouraging fleshy desires that will someday lead to death, and you will be responsible for that soul.

1 Corinthians 1:17 (NLT):

"For Christ didn't send me to baptize, but to preach the Good News—and not with clever speech, for fear that the cross of Christ would lose its power."

Would you look at that? Trying to be clever and inserting into the Gospel what God has not said weakens the message of the Cross. Of what use is a diluted Gospel? The Word of God is ENOUGH to save. **'It is the POWER of God at work, saving everyone who believes' Romans 1:16 (NLT).** Preach what the Bible has said. That is enough.

Jesus was not afraid to call out Pharisees or scatter the temple when needed; neither should you be. However, follow the leading of the Spirit when you do the work of God, not your pride or provocation. Love ultimately loves the Lord and seeks to please Him and only Him.

Once, as a new believer, I was what you'd call a *gay apologist*. I felt that as long as gay people were not harming anyone, they were not sinning. Maybe everyone else should leave them be. Then one day, I came across **Romans 1:26-27**; before that time, I had never seen it in the Bible that such was a sin. Ever since then, I have never made any excuses for them.

> 'One thing the devil has managed to do in our generation is making people sympathetic to things they should abominate.'
>
> - Pastor Emmanuel Iren

I have not seen it better put anywhere. If you loved someone, I believe you would want to lead them to the right path, not let them dwell in their wrong doing. Your parents did not let you do what was wrong because it was fun to you, they disciplined you because it was necessary for you to become a better human - THAT IS LOVE.

Romans 1:32 (NLT):

'**They know God's justice requires that those who do these things deserve to die, yet they do them anyway. Worse yet, they encourage others to do them, too.**'

Keeping quiet when you should speak up is lending your voice. It is a form of encouragement. Here is what you should do instead:

Ephesians 5:11 (NLT):

'**Take no part in the worthless deeds of evil and darkness; instead, expose them.**'

It should go without saying that this is no call to be unkind or condemn people. Love is at the core of everything you do as a Christian. Speaking the truth is no call to be mean or unkind.

Preach what is true. If you are not sure of the truth, check your Bible. It is the ultimate cheat code. Remember, judgement starts from the house of God:

1 Peter 4:17 (NLT):

'**For the time has come for judgment, and it must begin with God's household.**'

You are accountable to God whether you preach the Gospel or fail to do so. Please do not take it lightly. Eternity is at stake. It is literally a matter of life and death.

I pray the Holy Spirit leads you as you embark on this eternal journey of spreading the Word of salvation to the ends of the earth—in Jesus' Name. Amen.

Journal prompt:

Take a deep breath at this point. This chapter is lengthy for a good cause, I promise. One question I'd like you to answer is this: if you do not evangelise, what is the reason you haven't? If you evangelise, how can you do better and take the Gospel to more people? From this chapter, what keys will you be implementing first to kickstart or continue your journey?

Colossians 1:9-10 (NIV) -

'...continually ask God to fill you with the knowledge of his will through all the wisdom and understanding that the Spirit gives. So that you may live a life worthy of the Lord and please him in every way: bearing fruit in every good work, growing in the knowledge of God.'

Confession: I agree that I am created for His good purpose and that my life serves as a chariot for the swift movement of the Gospel. My heart is open, my hands are willing, and my feet are quick to go where You will send me, Abba—in Jesus' Name. Amen.

Evangelism is a must for every Christian. If you do not evangelise, what is the reason you haven't? If you evangelise, how can you do better and take the Gospel to more people? What steps will you take to use the keys provided in this chapter? Write two people you will start with and the date you will do it.

_____

_____

_____

_____

_____

_____

_____

_____

_____

_____

_____

_____

_____

_____

_____

_____

_____

_____

10

The Devil's Pandora's Box

John 8:44 (NIV) - *'You belong to your father, the devil, and you want to carry out your father's desires. He was a murderer from the beginning, not holding to the truth, for there is no truth in him. When he lies, he speaks his native language, for he is a liar and the father of lies.'*

The devil is first a liar and everything else afterwards. Keep this at the back and front of your mind and you will thank yourself for doing so. Do you know what Jesus says about His sheep? **'My sheep listen to my voice; I know them, and they follow me.' (John 10:27, NLT).**

God is firm and authoritative but NEVER unkind. This contrasts with what the devil sounds like. He is a liar and deceiver, attempting to mimic the voice of the Lord, but true knowledge of God will always keep you one step ahead. Studying the Word is so important. The more time you spend in God's presence, the more you can differentiate His voice from the million others trying to get in your head. Listen to His voice. Listen.

I once saw an Instagram post where a man said he always does the opposite of what the devil says, and it had me smiling. Trust me; the devil is not that smart. He only speaks from what God has already said. Go the opposite direction of what he says, and you will find the truth.

That being said, the devil's Pandora's Box is this - LIES.

I call it his Pandora's Box because every other evil he does always stems from a lie; '**...did God say you should not eat all the trees in the garden?' (Genesis 3:1)**; the first lie to man. In this instance, what he did was assign a different definition to death; while God saw death as the consequence of the knowledge of good and evil, which leads to both physical and spiritual death as well as separation from Him, the devil translated death to only mean the immediate physical kind. Eve believed, but that is not why we are here (actually, it is why we are here!)

Back on track, the devil starts from a lie. I do not want to plant images of a red, two-horned beast in your mind - and I'm sure the devil does not remotely look like that - but the Bible teaches that we cannot and are not ignorant of the wiles of the devil. (**2 Corinthians 2:11**). The devil always has trickery up his sleeves and one of the most common is *being oblivious*; that is why these 'lies' of the devil are the things your flesh may associate as 'normal' but they're not. That is just a narrative being pushed by the devil.

For this reason, the ongoing battle between your flesh - once subject to the world's influence under the tyranny of the devil - and your spirit - now locked and in sync with the Holy Spirit - continues as long as you live in this world. When you consider that you have desires that align with the Holy Spirit but sometimes derail to the side of your flesh, you will know that this goes beyond just 'feelings.' There is a constant war going on. If there was not, there would be no need for armour.

Ephesians 6:11-18 (KJV):

11 'Put on the whole armour of God, that ye may be able to stand against the wiles of the devil.

12 For we wrestle not against flesh and blood, but against principalities, against powers, against the rulers of the darkness of this world, against spiritual wickedness in high places.

13 Wherefore take unto you the whole armour of God, that ye may be able to withstand in the evil day, and having done all, to stand.

14 Stand therefore, having your loins girt about with truth, and having on the breastplate of righteousness

15 And your feet shod with the preparation of the gospel of peace;

16 Above all, taking the shield of faith, wherewith ye shall be able to quench all the fiery darts of the wicked.

17 And take the helmet of salvation, and the sword of the Spirit, which is the word of God:

18 Praying always with all prayer and supplication in the Spirit, and watching thereunto with all perseverance and supplication for all saints'

The armour prepares you for and protects you in battle. You should never be without it.

If there is one thing that evangelism has taught me, it is this: many people are just misinformed about the things of God. They believe they cannot get - in God - the things they can get in the world. That is just some *hot dodo*[24]. You and I know that it is not true, but that is the lie the devil spreads. Through evangelism, the right way, we can teach them that they can get all they need and even more!

Let me show you something that opened my mind to the truth of this.

2 Corinthians 4:3-4 (NIV) goes:

3 'And even if our gospel is veiled, it is veiled to those who are perishing.

4 The god of this age has blinded the minds of unbelievers, so that they cannot see the light of the gospel that displays the glory of Christ, who is the image of God.'

---

[24] *a blatant lie*

You see that?! God has done all He will do for us to save us. He has left His throne, come down as the man, Jesus, and sacrificed himself to pay for our sins. There is nothing more to do; the only thing left is that we ACCEPT Him and then begin the journey into the kingdom of Heaven as He continuously prunes us. The ones we call unbelievers are simply those who have not accepted this gift of salvation - not because they do not want to but because they may not know its value or cannot comprehend it.

It takes a man aware of his guilt and deserved punishment to appreciate a pardon from the judge; many *world people*[25] do not even know that being born into this world, being of Adam's seed, is THE sole qualification needed for condemnation—which is why salvation is necessary for every man. **Verse 3** in the above Scripture lets us know that the Gospel is only veiled to those whose minds have been blinded by the god of this world!

Nobody in their right mind would see something good and not want to have it - unless they do not know that it is good. The parable, describing the kingdom of heaven and comparing it to a man who found a treasure in a land goes:

Matthew 13:44 (NLT):

'The Kingdom of Heaven is like a treasure that a man discovered hidden in a field. In his excitement, he hid it again and sold everything he owned to get enough money to buy the field.'

---

[25] A pop culture expression for unbelievers

Just look at that. Only a person who knows the worth of a treasure can sell everything he has to get it. It is because we Christians have discovered heaven's worth, that we can give up the world for it. It is found without cost but attained with everything that you have.

So, you and I must evangelise, God's burden must be the burden of His children. We must preach and live the Gospel, even as we intercede for the lost, praying that God opens their eyes to His marvellous light. They need to know that *PAPA IS THE COOLEST!*

1 Corinthians 13:4-8 (NIV):

4 'Love is patient, love is kind. It does not envy, it does not boast, it is not proud.

5 It does not dishonour others, it is not self-seeking, it is not easily angered, it keeps no record of wrongs.

6 Love does not delight in evil but rejoices with the truth.

7 It always protects, always trusts, always hopes, always perseveres.

8 Love never fails. But where there are prophecies, they will cease; where there are tongues, they will be stilled; where there is knowledge, it will pass away.'

Replace 'love' with 'God,' who does not want that? I know I want that!!

Attached to this lie that one cannot get in God, what they get in the world is the **F**ear **O**f **M**issing **O**ut (**FOMO**), which the devil has used to hold many in his grip. I will not dwell much on this because I want you to know only one thing - IF YOU ARE IN GOD'S WILL FOR YOUR LIFE, YOU ARE CERTAINLY NOT MISS-ING OUT ON ANYTHING THE WORLD HAS TO OFFER. Even if there was anything to miss out on, is it from this world that barely knows its left from its right? *Biko.*

Another lie I often encounter is the belief that this world is all there is; and if it is not, there is time to repent eventually. As a kid, I watched many Nollywood movies where dying people would repent on their deathbeds and make it to Heaven. Would you believe it if I told you that repeatedly seeing those scenes planted a mindset that made me begin to pray to God that if I die, it should not be a quick or immediate death so I can *quickly* give my life to Christ? I am sure you can relate. What this lie does is that it makes people do all they can to be the best in this world, setting their eyes on fame, wealth, and others of that ilk while assigning Christianity to the last few minutes of their lives. Thank God for His mercy.

You and I know that this world is little of what is. Real life is eternal life and we are just here to prepare for a place we should have been in all along if not for sin. The marriage of the bride to the bridegroom is what we look forward to! **(Revelations 19:6-9).**

Today's world has many professions that many people feel Christians should not do or cannot be involved in and succeed. We have many instances of musicians who started in the church but eventually left. There is the notion that you cannot get to certain heights in your career if you are a Christian since you cannot play dirty; a ready example of this is politics. This is also just another lie of the devil.

Now, while it may seem like the game is rigged - and I do agree that it is NOT everything that a Christian can agree to do, sacrifices must be made for this Godly lifestyle - the real question is this, *'Are you doing what you do for God's glory or your own?'* If you are doing what you are doing for God and the Gospel, I assure you that fame or money will be the least of your problems. Glorify God, and He will glorify you. The only difference between what you do for God and what you do for the devil is who gets the glory.

'What is in your hand?' Everything that is not a sin can be used for God's glory. Remember, the devil can only pervert the good stuff God has made. God always gives richly for our enjoyment **(1 Timothy 6:17)**.

Your talent, whether you sing, dance, act, or play football…it can be used for God's glory. But many people do not know this. Many people have The Disconnect planted in their minds, so they cannot reconcile all parts of their lives to God. But through you, God's light in the dark, you can show them how, especially now that you have read this book.

Do Christians think small?

Luke 16: 8-9 (NIV):

8 'The master commended the dishonest manager because he had acted shrewdly. For the people of this world are shrewder in dealing with their own kind than are the people of the light.

9 I tell you, use worldly wealth to gain friends for yourselves, so that when it is gone, you will be welcomed into eternal dwellings.'

The shrewd manager's parable is one that puzzled me at first. It told the story of a dishonest manager who was about to be fired so he quickly curried favour from his master's clients by reducing the debts they owed and when he eventually got fired, he had enough connections to fall back on and start over. The MSG translation is where you want to read it from.

Luke 16:8-9 (MSG):

'Now here's a surprise: The master praised the crooked manager! And why? Because he knew how to look after himself. Streetwise people are smarter in this regard than law-abiding citizens. They are on constant alert, looking for angles, surviving by their wits. I want you to be smart in the same way—but for what is right—using every adversity to stimulate you to creative survival, to concentrate your attention on the bare essentials, so you'll live, really live, and not complacently just get by on good behaviour.'

Many believers unconsciously live life in a very timid manner. They think it is okay to live a small life: to be okay with having little; to not do too much; to be as unnoticeable as possible. Just be on their best behaviour and quote Scriptures every two seconds, if possible. There is nothing wrong with these, but that is the bare minimum, in my opinion, and should go without saying since you are a Christian.

Jesus, in this parable, enjoins us to be smart in the same way as the shrewd servant but in light of what benefits the kingdom of God. So be on constant alert and use material wealth to make connections for yourself in places that matter; if, like the shrewd servant, you can utilise material wealth properly, then surely you can handle kingdom wealth. Be creatively innovative, create solutions for people that will solve actual problems, be mature and make connections with a wide range of people outside your religious circles. You can be the influence of Christ in a place, in little or big ways. **Verse 10** of the same Scripture goes:

> **'Whoever can be trusted with very little can also be trusted with much, and whoever is dishonest with very little will also be dishonest with much.'**

Are you the kind that believes that you do not have enough to do much? I assure you, with everything inside (and outside) me, that is a lie from the pit of hell. If anything, the parable of the talents **(Matthew 25:14-30)** teaches that for every talent that God has deposited inside of you, He expects a yield or interest on it. He expects multiplication. Has he not put within you the ability to be fruitful and multiply? It goes beyond procreation.

How can you carry fire and be hidden? Where can light go if it does not want to be seen? The answer is nowhere. Unless, of course, you dim the light - which is what I have seen Christians do repeatedly. It was what I did, too.

When I got saved, the peace that enveloped me was so great, that I did not want to do anything but be in God's presence. You see, I was coming from a very dark place. I was coming from constant anxiety, hurt, and emotional damage. I had everything I wanted here. I did want to share the good news. However, I took a wrong turn by thinking that was all there was supposed to be. I did not see how my work, appearance, and dreams connected to the Gospel.

From the beginning, God gave Adam dominion, although the devil tried to circumvent that, Jesus restored us. While we focus on the eternal aspect of things, not being carnally minded, this earth is also ours for the taking, and we must take it. Since God is big, why are you thinking small?

This knowledge is not for everyone. You might not understand it today or in the next one or two years but I'm banking on the hope that one day, you will. I pray the Spirit opens the eyes of your understanding to grasp this truth.

Sucrée

One morning in the 'ember months of 2021, I woke up, and all I could think of was Sucrée. Sucrée was a business I'd started a year back but took a pause because of school. That morning, I believe the Holy Spirit showed me the connection between that dream of mine and the Gospel. I saw how starting up a business and achieving great things with it would bring influence to God's kingdom. I saw the picture clearly, and I am running with it till this day.

Do you, now, know? That you were made to do great things? Christians cannot afford to play it safe. We are made to be big thinkers, and why not? Consider that God has assured us that He will do *beyond* what we can think or dream **(Ephesians 3:20)**. I believe the real question here should be, *'how big can you dream?'* We kingdom people cannot afford to be still asking whether or not women should wear trousers when we should be looking to start businesses that advocate the Jesus Culture.

You cannot get by on 'good' behaviour when the workers are few and the harvest is ready. You cannot diminish your light when it's supposed to be the beacon that brings people to Christ. If Jesus has called you to be the light of the world, why are you content with only being the light of your street? If that isn't a call for children of God to have dominion over the world and its systems then I don't know what it is.

I went through many phases to get to this knowledge; many ideas I had were turned on their heads when confronted with the truth. With this book, you do not have to. I am here to tell you that you can do whatever, be that it gives glory to God. I do not mean you should do evil and say it gives glory to God **(Romans 3:7-8)**. Be wise, use your creativity, and innovate for the church. Use your wits for creative survival.

Be street smart for the kingdom. Compete on benchmarked standards—**because you're doing it for God is enough reason to do it better.** Whatever gift in you is for the world, not just your current location or state. You have an excellent spirit **(Daniel 5:12)**; whatever you do must be excellent. Don't restrict yourself with your imagination. What dream do you have? Hold on to it and see if God will not do it.

Do you even realise the Spirit of Whom is in you? Look at the skies and the stars, how we wake up every day to see the sun where it is supposed to be. Look at nature and how it restores its balance no matter how much it is shaken. Look at your skin and how you heal after an injury. Look at your hair. Look at your feet and toes. Have you ever looked at another human being and been like, 'Wow, so everything that I can do, feel and perceive, there is this whole other person with his own set of feelings and perceptions?' Now, let me blow your mind: the One who made ALL THESE THINGS, in whose hands the earth hangs; He lives INSIDE you, so you are CAPABLE of the same things because you are made in His image, and He has given you these abilities. WOW! If you have ever marvelled at a scientific invention or technological innovation, now you know THE source.

The biggest test of your faith is having audacity. *Dreaming big is thinking of the things that you know you cannot pull off by yourself because you expect God to show up.*

Terry Storch, one of the founders of YouVersion, puts it this way:

> 'We will never insult God with small thinking and safe living. Setting goals that are beyond the realm of possibility because you expect God to show up is having audacious expectations.'

- Scaling leadership Day 6[26].

Make no mistake, this sort of lifestyle is not for a group of Christians that we like to call 'Charismatic.' This lifestyle is for everyone who believes in Jesus. In that sense, every Christian should be charismatic. The Holy Spirit is the only charisma you will ever need and He is already inside you. Consider the Scripture, **1 Samuel 14 (NIV)**; the Israelites are in a war, and theirs is not the winning side. Jonathan, son of Saul, leaves the camp to go ahead to the enemy territory. He says in **verse 6:**

'Come, let's go over to the outpost of those uncircumcised men. Perhaps the Lord will act on our behalf. Nothing can hinder the Lord from saving, whether by many or by few.'

This is faith! Shown in works! Okay, you have prayed, but have you moved? Jonathan did not sit in the camp waiting for deliverance from God. He was a soldier, so he acted like one and provoked God to act. He said, *'it does not matter whether we are two men or two million; God will save us as long as we expect Him to show up.'* God did show up. Spectacularly.

---

[26] Terry Storch: *YouVersion Bible plan; Scaling leadership Day 6*

That is the kind of audacity that is backed by God. Dreaming big is expecting God to show up, but you must not just dream. You must show up too.

Influence for the Kingdom

God wants you to do things that haven't been done before. People often put evangelism within a box; do you think God's calling is restricted only to church planting? Churches are of maximum importance but so are systems that will allow Christianity to thrive in the state. As I write this, the current state of the world makes me wonder what Apostle Paul would write if he was alive in this time. Moses would not only shatter but crush the tablets to pieces. We not only need prophets and priests now; we need Christian founders, lawmakers, business owners, innovators, and more that will set up systems with God at the centre. We need to multiply the effectiveness of evangelism through influence and power.

Paul had powerful friends **(Acts 19:31)**, Jesus had powerful friends (Joseph of Arimathea), David had Jonathan, and Mordecai had Esther. God often creates allies for us in powerful places when we need them, but you can also become that influence, as we see in the stories of Joseph, the dreamer and later in Mordecai. It is important, especially for the Gospel. We can influence systems the right way.

We have a part to play in spreading the Gospel to the ends of the world before the end comes.

Matthew 24:14 (KJV):

'And this gospel of the kingdom shall be preached in all the world for a witness unto all nations; and then shall the end come.'

27/04/2022

It's the day Elon Musk acquired Twitter in April (or the news says he is going to). I am sitting at home with my gaze directed to the ceiling and head on the back of the chair, thinking random thoughts. My older sister, lying adjacent to me in the sitting room, says - to no one in particular as she scrolls through her phone - 'So Elon Musk has finally bought Twitter.' I shake my head, not concerned and then say out loud, 'Everyone and their own.' Almost immediately, the Holy Spirit corrects me. He says, 'No. He is making decisions that will affect you.'

I look down instantly to ensure I am not hearing from an outside source. This is enough to change my mind-set! And not just Elon Musk; powerful people are making decisions that will affect the whole world. These people's intentions are barely discernible because it is unclear what they're after (actually, it is quite discernible). Can you afford to stay on the side-lines?

I want to make something crystal clear - **influence is NOT the goal, the prevalence of the Gospel is THE goal, and influence is the tool.** Read that again. Consider God's Word to Baruch at a trying time in Israel.

He says in Jeremiah 45:5 (NIV):

'Should you then seek great things for yourself? Do not seek them. For I will bring disaster on all people, declares the Lord, but wherever you go I will let you escape with your life.'

A little back story - Baruch was Jeremiah's scribe who wrote down his prophecies and saw God at work, and he probably expected that these prophecies might bring him to some sort of attainment of personal ambition - whatever that may be. However, the opposite happened, and he was thrown into the dungeon with the prophet Jeremiah because Israel's king had hardened his heart against God **(Jeremiah 36 & 45)**. Baruch was fearful and sad because his expectations were not met, but God said that his desired greatness was unimportant! Above all, God would preserve his life.

We live in similar times, trying times. While you seek to be great and do great things for God, you must never hold on to them above your God. Never get attached to anything but the Gospel. Dear Light, travel light in this world.

You have authority

If only you knew how threatening you are - not just to the devil but - to the kingdom of darkness as a whole. How scared the devil is every time you open your mouth to pray or flip open the Scriptures to study it. If you did, you would smile to the battlefield of prayer! This is the authority that you have as a child of God.

Jesus calls us to participation; God, Himself, gave us an authority that even He does not argue with. See for yourself in **Genesis 2**, where He gave Adam the right to name animals and did not argue with any decision Adam made. Sin might have come to spoil that but Jesus has also come, to restore that right. We have the authority. You and I.

You have heard that the church is the body of Christ. This is true. Have you ever tied a rubber band tightly around your finger? What happens is that it is cut off from blood supply and will eventually die off if left that way for long enough. As Christians, we are supplying vessels to others in the body of Christ - when you do not perform in the capacity that you should for the Gospel, you hinder the body of Christ.

Ephesians 3:18 - 20 (NIV) goes:

18 'That we may have power, together with all the Lord's holy people, to grasp how wide and long and high and deep is the love of Christ,

19 and to know this love that surpasses knowledge—that you may be filled to the measure of all the fullness of God.

20 Now to him who is able to do immeasurably more than all we ask or imagine, according to his power that is at work within us,'

This love, shown on the cross, makes all we want in Christ possible. This love is the authority that we have. **Colossians 1:10 (NIV)** calls us to: 'live a life worthy of the Lord and please him in every way: bearing fruit in every good work, growing in the knowledge of God.' This is possible when we are filled with the knowledge of God's will. To be filled with this knowledge that feeds and assures you of your authority means constantly being in His presence and being in on what our Lord is doing. Staying connected to your source is not negotiable

The Midas Touch

As a child of God, who has influence, people will want your opinion on things; marriage, relationships, and business. It may seem wrong because they should look to the Word, instead, but it is your chance to get them around to the way of God. Let your opinion stem from the Word in all you do. **Titus 2:1 (NLT)** say **'As for you, Titus, promote the kind of living that reflects wholesome teaching.'** Let your lifestyle reflect the Word of God in you.

Have you heard the story of Midas? He wanted all he touched to become gold, but that had its consequences as he turned his child to gold, too. These consequences do not apply to Christians, at least not in the way it did for Midas. Everything you touch WILL turn to gold one way or the other by the power of the Holy Ghost. You will walk into a room and flood it with light. **'Nations will come to your light, And kings to the brightness of your rising (Isaiah 60:3, AMP).** People will say, **'Let us go with you, for we have heard that God is with you.'** **(Zechariah 8:23, CSB).** This is what we mean when we sing, *'Anyone I touch, surely must be blessed.*[27]' Surely, this is even worth more than gold!

So, start dreaming. Do it big, and do not stop when you wake up. God will show up for your precious dreams, every single one of them.

The devil may have his box full of lies but you have the Word full of TRUTH. It is certain who is winning the war.

---

[27] A line from a common song, often energetic and demonstrative in rendition

Journal prompt:

Ponder over all you have just read. What is at the back of your mind right now? Are there any lies you used to hold on to concerning being a Christian or dreaming big? The Holy Spirit is tearing down every knowledge that exalts itself about the knowledge of God in your life. Head to your journal and pour out your heart, God is listening to you, and He is ready to partner with you and make your dreams come true.

John 8:44 (NIV) -

'You belong to your father, the devil, and you want to carry out your father's desires. He was a murderer from the beginning, not holding to the truth, for there is no truth in him. When he lies, he speaks his native language, for he is a liar and the father of lies.'

Confession: I must remember that the devil is a liar and that whatever he says is untrue. Therefore, I tear down every imagination or wrong mindset that exalts itself against the knowledge of God in my life. The devil's lies have no bearing over the truth of God in my life. I will do all that God will have me do, where He will have me do it and I will lead others to their deliverance by virtue of this truth—in Jesus' Name. Amen.

(insert your name), *the dreamer: Write down your dreams. Everything you ever thought you could be or do. Write them down here, don't hold back, this is between you and Abba.*

_____

_____

_____

_____

_____

_____

_____

_____

_____

_____

_____

_____

_____

_____

_____

_____

_____

_____

_____

11

The Master Key

Old Sunday school number -

'Prayer is the key
Prayer is the key
Prayer is the master key!
Jesus started with prayer
And ended with prayer
Prayer is the master key.'

I sang this song many times in church, and only recently did I begin to grasp the true meaning of these words. I feel that prayer is taken too lightly and trivially among believers, today. Yes, God is your friend, but He is also the Master of the universe. Reverence is indispensable.

Prayer, today, has been reduced to the art of asking God rather than aligning with the will of God. Prayer is a power at the disposal of every believer for the sake of spreading the gospel.

The Word enjoins us thus:

Ephesians 6:18 (KJV)

18 'Praying always with all prayer and supplication in
the Spirit, and watching thereunto with all perseverance
and supplication for all saints;'

You should pray ALWAYS. With ALL kinds of prayer; prayers of
worship **(Hebrews 13:15)**, prayers of faith **(James 5:13-16)**, prayers
of thanksgiving **(Psalms 100:4)**, prayers of intercession **(Daniel
9:1-27)**, corporate prayers **(Acts 12:5-18)**, prayers of consecration
(Matthew 20:26-27) - all led by the Holy Spirit **(Romans 8:26-
27)**. With ALL perseverance and continuity, never ceasing **(Luke
18:1, 1 Thessalonians 5:17)**. For ALL saints.

My dad always says that praying is like building a monument or
a skyscraper. The higher you want to build or mount, the deeper the
foundation must be. In the same way, your prayer life must be deep
if you want to connect with the dreams that God has for you and
fulfil your purpose. In other words, the more you pray, the better.
You can never pray too much.

In evangelism, prayer is indispensable. Without prayer, it is simply impossible. I said earlier that God has done all that He could
possibly do to save mankind. What is left is that this gift of salvation
is accepted by mankind. But it is not always the case.

2 Corinthians 4:4 (KJV):

4 'In whom the god of this world hath blinded the minds
of them which believe not, lest the light of the glorious

gospel of Christ, who is the image of God, should shine unto them.'

Why the gift of salvation has not been accepted by many is because their minds are closed by the devil, and they cannot see the light of the Gospel. I have spoken to people who believe that the devil does not exist and that Christians are being too superstitious about him. If indeed the god of this world (the devil) has blinded their minds, it is not far-fetched that they would think in this manner, is it?

The devil's hold on this world was gotten from Adam when he ate the forbidden fruit. If the devil did not have such power, he certainly would not have offered it to Jesus as a temptation.

Luke 4:5-7 (NLT):

5 'Then the devil took him up and revealed to him all the kingdoms of the world in a moment of time.

6 I will give you the glory of these kingdoms and authority over them," the devil said, "because THEY ARE MINE TO GIVE TO ANYONE I PLEASE.

7 I will give it all to you if you will worship me.'

But Jesus knew that while such an offer was valid, it was also temporary. Satan's lease on this world is not forever, which is why he wants to gather as many men with him to his judgement. However, that is not God's will for man. God's will is plainly stated:

2 Peter 3:9 (NLT):

9 '...He does not want anyone to be destroyed, but wants everyone to repent.'

As believers, we partner with God to carry out His will. The reason for this is that God is not a dictator. For His will to be done, SOMEBODY must want that to happen.

It is why you and I must pray that the eyes of people will be open to God's light. God seeks out intercessors to stand and pray for the lost so they may be saved.

Ezekiel 22:30-31 (NLT):

30 'I looked for someone who might rebuild the wall of righteousness that guards the land. I searched for someone to stand in the gap in the wall so I wouldn't have to destroy the land, but I found no one.

31 So now I will pour out my fury on them, consuming them with the fire of my anger. I will heap on their heads the full penalty for all their sins. I, the Sovereign Lord, have spoken!'

The consequence of sin is judgement but an intercessor can make all the difference, resulting in mercy, instead. God saves many people daily because of the prayer of one saint. He would have spared the decadent city of Sodom and Gomorrah for the sake of Abraham if He had found 10 righteous men **(Genesis 18:16-33)**. Will you stand in the gap? You can…through prayer!

Pray Persistently

In matters like this (evangelism), and even others as we are led by the Holy Spirit, we must persist in prayer. Jesus taught this through the parable of the persistent widow who continued to seek justice from an unjust judge until she got it. Jesus said that if a partial judge could give fair judgement to the widow just because she persisted, how much more will God, who is just and righteous, answer His children without delay? **(Luke 18:1-8)**. **In the same way, prayer requires persistence and not just persistence for answers but your alignment to the will of God.**

Why persist in prayer? Because it is a war for the most precious thing in this world - SOULS. You need to wake up! The verses you like to recite from **Ephesians 6:11-18** about putting on the **'full armour of God'** are not just verbal declarations but confessions that lead you into battle - you need to pray more!

If you are in a battlefield, you would not hit your enemy and run off, hoping he won't come after you. You would make sure that your enemy never gets the chance to attack you again. You would do this through any means possible because it is a matter of life and death. In the same way, realise that you fight as you pray (remember it is the armour of God and armours are only required in a time of battle), so you cannot give up so easily. You must pray till your enemy lays cold on the hard floor; until the answer comes forth.

By 'enemy', I do not mean your village people[28] or that person who you think is against your progress. Addictive habits, wrong mindsets, wrong knowledge and wrong belief systems are also enemies to the will of God in your life and these enemies must be defeated. These were what Apostle Paul referred to in **2 Corinthians 10:4-5 (NLT)** as he expounded on the spiritual power available to Christians by the Holy Ghost, He said, **'We use God's mighty weapons, not worldly weapons, to knock down the STRONG-HOLDS OF HUMAN REASONING and to destroy false arguments. We destroy every proud obstacle that keeps people from knowing God. We capture their REBELLIOUS THOUGHTS and teach them to obey Christ.'** Wrong human reasoning are strongholds against the will of God too! Now even if there are actually people you *feel* are working against you, it is wise to know that beyond human enmity, it is the devil working through them that you should pray against. **'For we wrestle not against flesh and blood, but against principalities, against powers, against the rulers of the darkness of this world, against spiritual wickedness in high places' (Ephesians 6:12, KJV).** The kingdom of darkness has not stopped striving against God's children since the time of Daniel, neither should we stop praying.

---

[28] In common conversations and pop culture, this phrase refers to the myth that persons from one's ancestral land are responsible for misfortune, hardship or coincidental traits of bad luck.

When persisting, you must also know that what we humans perceive as a 'delay' in receiving answers from God or God not hearing us when we pray is often a case of our inability *to see - with our physical eyes - the process that God has initiated to answer our prayer.* The God who gave you ears is not deaf, He can hear! Whatever God desires to give you is good and may take time because God always gives what will last. His blessings are not fleeting or temporary. God may not always be 'early', but He is always **on time**. You must trust this as you persist in prayer. You must trust that God knows what He is doing, because HE DOES!

Persistence requires faith. By what other means would a widow keep going to a judge who had told her 'no' countless times? **(Luke 18:1-5)**. That's faith! As a Christian, faith is not foolish hope or a 'maybe,' it is the **'...evidence of things not seen' (Hebrews 11:1)** and a non-negotiable feature of persistent prayer. You don't have faith because you believe before what you pray for happens; you believe because what you pray for has already happened so you must act like it. Then, you keep praying into its physical manifestation. **'You can pray for anything, and if you have faith, you will receive it' (Matthew 21:22 NLT)**.

You must have *faith* to *pray persistently*, else, it would be an exercise in futility. The Amplified version does justice to **Hebrews 11:1**; it says, **'faith comprehends as fact what cannot be experienced by the physical senses.'** WOW! That verse is simply saying that your physical senses: your sight, your sense of smell or touch are not anything to go by when it comes to the matter of faith—which is required for prayer. It cannot be experienced by your physical senses. Therefore, look to your spirit!

Did you see Jesus die? Did you see Him resurrect? Did you see any of the disciples? How then, do you know that all these happened? How do you know that you are saved? It is by faith! **Romans 8:16 (NLT)** says that '**For his Spirit joins with our spirit to affirm that we are God's children.**' The affirmation of your belief that you are a child of God - upon receiving salvation - is by God's Spirit to your spirit. It is a spiritual thing! This strong faith which is the foundation of your belief in Christ is the same kind of faith that you must employ as you persist in prayer or pray any kind of prayer. You may not see, but your spirit SEES. You may not know, but your spirit KNOWS. Why? Because your spirit is connected to His Spirit since you are His child. In time, you will experience the physical manifestation of what has already happened in the spirit.

So, persist. Keep at prayer, even when the results are not apparent to you yet in the physical. Spend time praying, don't put yourself in a box concerning the amount of time you want to spend praying, pray for as long as you have to. **Keep at prayer, not just for certain answers to the things you want but for an alignment to the will of God.** Keep at prayer, because it keeps you from temptation (**Matthew 26:41**). Keep at prayer, so that the ones whose sights have been taken by the devil (**2 Corinthians 4:4**) can begin to see God's light and be saved. Don't stop praying, because Jesus, your Master, commands it (**Luke 18:1**).

Pray for Nations

1 Timothy 2:1-4 (KJV):

1 'I exhort therefore, that, first of all, supplications, prayers, intercessions, and giving of thanks, be made for all men;

2 For kings, and for all that are in authority; that we may lead a quiet and peaceable life in all godliness and honesty.

3 For this is good and acceptable in the sight of God our Saviour;

4 Who will have all men to be saved, and to come unto the knowledge of the truth.'

It is much harder to spread the Gospel in nations with wars or daunting circumstances. In nations where ruthless leaders are in positions of power, Christianity goes into hiding. For us to lead peaceful lives in all godliness and for Christianity to keep prevailing, our intercession for ALL in authority is very important.

It is bad enough that people have been blinded to the truth of the Gospel. Worse is where policies are implemented to discourage people from being Christian(s). So, pray for your country, the leaders, and all those in positions of power. It is not enough to talk about how problematic the world and the nations of the world are and go home with a serious headache and dry throat; PRAY.

The WORD

Hebrews 4:12-13 (MSG):

'God means what he says. What he says goes. His powerful Word is sharp as a surgeon's scalpel, cutting through everything, whether doubt or defence, laying us open to listen and obey. Nothing and no one can resist God's Word. We can't get away from it—no matter what.'

The Bible forms our knowledge of God; it's a manual that you cannot do without so you do not give place to error in your life. In the Word, you discover who you are and what you can do in God. The Word lays us open to listen and obey. We have our hearts laid bare and can unlearn our many errors while accepting His truth. Many Christians act based on good intentions rather than what God's word says. This leads to error and can be fatal.

2 Timothy 2:15 (KJV):

'Study to shew thyself approved unto God, a workman that needeth not to be ashamed, rightly dividing the word of truth.'

We study God's word because how else can we provide the defence for our faith when we are asked? (1 Peter 3:15). Since the Word is God, it means that whenever we turn the pages of our Bibles, we learn another aspect of Abba. It means we look at Him, gazing at His many facets to discover more and more of who He is so we can know who we are since we are made in His image. It means that through the Word, we can truly know ourselves.

Priesthood

Revelation 1:5-6 (KJV):

5 'And from Jesus Christ, who is the faithful witness, and the first begotten of the dead, and the prince of the kings of the earth. Unto him that loved us, and washed us from our sins in his own blood,

6 And hath made us kings and priests unto God and his Father; to him be glory and dominion for ever and ever. Amen.'

We're all anointed as priests, as people who stand in the gap. Praying is the job of every Christian. Through prayer, we birth things into this world, we decree things and they come to pass. We pray for the ones who cannot, for the ones who are lost that they may see His light, for the ones who are ignorant of their power in God.

We pray for ALL, ALL the time. Prayer is not restricted to specific seasons or times or when your local church declares a special prayer program. No, prayer is all day, every day. Prayer is for life.

By the Spirit

Above all, by the Spirit. It would be fruitless to try to provoke the things of God by the flesh. God's leading must come first - or else, all efforts would be in vain.

John 16:13 (MSG):

13 'the Spirit of the Truth, he will take you by the hand and guide you into all the truth there is. He won't draw attention to himself, but will make sense out of what is about to happen and, indeed, out of all that I (Jesus) have done and said.'

Trust the leading of the Spirit in all that you do from praying to studying the Word to dreaming big and spreading the Gospel. I pray that the Spirit continues to reveal His truth to you—in Jesus' Name. Amen.

Journal prompt:

In what way can you begin to upgrade your prayer life?

1 Thessalonians 5:17 (KJV) -

'Pray without ceasing.'

Confession: I declare that my mouth is a mouthpiece for the kingdom. I declare and bring things to pass. My prayers are effective—in Jesus' Name. Amen.

What can you do to make your prayer life better? Write them down - off the top of your head. Start with those small changes and let them add up as you remain consistent.

_____

_____

_____

_____

_____

_____

_____

_____

_____

_____

_____

_____

_____

_____

_____

_____

_____

_____

12

Being the Light

Matthew 5:14 (NIV) - *'You are the light of the world. A town built on a hill cannot be hidden.'*

Being the light means being an all-rounder. It means walking into a room and **illuminating** it. I am living proof that people may not be so interested in the Word of God, but many things about your lifestyle - fuelled by the light of God - can pull them towards you. It can be anything from your amazing dress sense or how well you speak; it all adds up for the kingdom. This is why you must actively develop yourself. It was not until I started to run a Christian community that I realised I was terrible at public speaking - using too many filler words and speaking too fast. What did I do? I recorded myself speaking, played it back, and took points to improve it.

Your personal development is essential for your well-being and the Gospel. When Jesus enjoined us to let our light shine, He added a reason, that people would see **'your good works and give glory to your Father in heaven'** (Matthew 5:16, CSB).

The knowledge you have is not what makes you stand out. What makes you stand out are the works that this knowledge makes you perform. People do not give glory to God simply because you are a Christian, but when you are a Christian, whose life is complete in every way by the power of the Gospel, those are evident works that provoke even unbelievers to worship your God.

Doing this is the first step to changing the stereotypical notions that many unbelievers and even believers have about what a Christian should look like. I remember having a conversation with a stranger, and at the end of it, when we exchanged Instagram handles, he was so shocked that I was a Christian. In his words, I looked and sounded too cool to be religious. It was funny, but many people still have that image of long shirts and longer skirts when they think of Christians. This, in itself, is not bad; the effects, however, can be. When people have a certain mindset of how things should be, it influences what they think about it and their response to it, impacting their receptiveness to the Gospel.

In this day and age when there exist many 'Christian' sects that promise hell fire for people who look a certain way or wear certain things, it is crucial that people know that they do not have to be a certain way or look a certain way to qualify as Christians. **All you have to be is LIGHT.** The kind Jesus inspires you to be. The kind that the Holy Spirit teaches you to be. Pure and Holy. A beacon of hope. If you can be like this, it will change the shallow idea that many people have of Christianity. They will know that the Christian lifestyle is true freedom because where the Spirit is, there - alone - can freedom reign.

A light is put where it will shine the most; this advocates amplification. Ask yourself, *'how can I be better?'* If you know the child of Whom you are, you will know that you cannot afford to settle or accept that *'that's just the way I am.' Mbanu*[29].

How do you actively develop yourself?

1. *Extend your focus beyond purely religious aspects of life:*

While there might be the temptation to read only your Bible for the rest of your life and watch solely Christian movies, there are many materials out there that will broaden your knowledge horizon and sharpen your mind; books or materials about entrepreneurship, building, self-development, history, and many more. Doing this will also help you to have priceless knowledge (which is power) and to hold intelligent conversations that do not solely revolve around spirituality.

One thing I know about me is that I have been reading right from my mother's womb. An incident that happened when I was much younger proves this - I mistakenly locked my father's key inside his room because I was reading a book while closing the door and did not realise my mistake until much later. Of course, he was angry, but two weeks later, he was beaming with pride as he related the story to my class teacher during the open day as proof of what an intelligent daughter he has. Parents, *rolls eyes*...to think that he almost shouted off my head that day.

---

[29] Igbo Word meaning *No*

Anyways, back here, reading has been my armour for as long as I know. Bring up any topic, and I have something to say about it, even if it is just a little information. It is important to, and it is not everywhere that you can directly speak Scripture, but you can astutely make references to it like Paul did sagaciously in **Acts 17** to let people know where you belong. Know other things too. Can you have a good conversation? Can you convince a person with your words? Can you properly articulate your thoughts? All these things are what reading extensively will teach you.

My point is that information is really powerful. Wisdom is the application of knowledge, meaning you apply what you know. While I sternly advocate for books because I love them so much, technology has made information much easier to access through podcasts, videos, audiobooks, and more. Take advantage of these.

In doing this, be careful that you do not consume the things that will corrupt your mind. There are books you may not have the maturity to read or do not even need to read. Why? I once read a book on Demonology purely out of curiosity back when I was not saved; however, my long experience reading has made it possible for me to dissect truth from the untrue easily, and these sorts of things do not affect me in a way they may affect another person - or so I like to think. Still, there is some information you do not need - just like that book up there.

Base everything upon the truth of the Word. Your learning and experiences must run through the filter of the Word. Doing this will enable you to process the real truths of situations and circumstances when confronted with a lie.

Be extensive. Study wide. Do research. Know how things work. Be curious as guided by the Holy Spirit.

2. Keep the kingdom in sight:

As you try to be extensive, keep a goal in mind. Do not just consume anything for consumption's sake. That would be dangerous and give an inroad to the devil. Do not overestimate your 'control' over anything. There are some things you should gladly 'flee' from **(1 Peter 5:8-9).**

There must be unity of purpose for the kingdom in whatever you do. Whether you study psychology to understand how people think or read *48 Laws of Power*[30] to understand the workings and dynamics of power, know why you do it, and heavenly wisdom will help you apply that knowledge. You are not doing it to manipulate people or to corrupt your mind. You are doing it for the kingdom of God and for the furtherance of the Gospel.

3. Connect the dots because they always do:

One thing that being extensive in developing myself has helped me do is connect the dots; by this, I mean that everything in life is interrelated in some way. I can read the Bible and see how everything else in life connects to it. It can be mind-blowing because it helps me realise how CONSISTENT God has been from the start. No single shifting shadows. None **(James 1:17).**

---

[30] *48 Laws of Power by* Robert Greene

Learn to connect the dots. How? Examine whatever you do and inquire how it connects back to God. From your work, your hobbies, your communication, your actions, your talents; if you can perceive how everything in your life connects with one another and back to God, you will never walk outside the lane of purpose. You will truly be a light because men and women will find God through your works.

4. Be self-aware. Practice:

Know 'YOU'; with the help of the Spirit, you can. The Word (Jesus) is a revealer of intents and purposes, but through self-deceit, you can read the Bible all year and see only what you choose to see. Therefore, let the Holy Spirit reveal the issues in your heart to you so that you can work on your flaws which hinder you from accepting His truths. The more you yield, the more self-aware you will be.

5. Choose excellence in all you do, always:

If He has indeed given an excellent spirit, this should be relatively easy. Choose to excel, even in those things that are seemingly inconsequential.

Salvation is the best thing that has ever happened to humanity, and it will often set off character and personal development, but that development is something that you must yearn for and be conscious about undertaking. You have to figure that out yourself. Know your traumas and what sets you off. Try to be better every day than you were the day before. Ask the Holy Spirit to reveal your desires to you, correct your ideologies, and dethrone any knowledge that conflicts with the knowledge of God in your life.

2 Corinthians 10:5 (NIV)

'**We demolish arguments and every pretension that sets itself up against the knowledge of God, and we take captive every thought to make it obedient to Christ.**'

It will be painful, but it will be worth it. How else can gold be refined except through the fire?

Listen,

Jesus says a lamp will be put where it can give the most light. I beg you, do not diminish any part of yourself because you are trying to live 'right.' Right is not always conservative or any other term designed to qualify it. Right is light, the light God has called you to be.

God has called you to be light. It means that you stand in stark contrast to the culture of this world. That means non-conformity to the standards of this world just like **Romans 12:2** rightly says. Hold on to your faith. Be glad to 'miss out' on the things of this world.

Noah, Moses, Elijah, Jesus, and many other people in the Bible stood as light against the prevailing systems of the world in their times and faced tremendous trials. Still, they stood. It will be the same for you if you so desire. If you can hold on to your faith. If you can continuously stand for what is right.

Philippians 2:15 (NLT):

'...Live clean, innocent lives as children of God, shining like bright lights in a world full of crooked and perverse people.'

God desires that you prosper in every way and be His star in this dark world. God doesn't do mediocrity. Check the Word.

Jireh wants you to live a full life. He does. Having bad habits when it comes to your health and well-being is doing a disservice to yourself. Looking or presenting yourself as less than you are will chase away people that should be coming toward you.

These things actually matter. They do. Fix it up, brethren.

This is evangelism, too. The greatest miracle is that His Spirit is in you, not just resting on you like in the Old Testament. What can you not do?

Love

Love is the greatest of them all. It is the ultimate spiritual maturity: an acceptance of the possibility of the worst a person can be, like God does for us. When you consider this love God has for us, right from the beginning of time, don't you want to do great things for Him?

If you love God, such is displayed for Him in obedience. Jesus, Himself, said that if we love Him, we will keep His commands **(John 14:15).** More than screaming, 'we love Him', we must answer *'Here I am,'* when He asks, *'Who will I send?'* **(Isaiah 6:8).**

The love and compassion of Jesus had Him moved by the crowds, healing all wherever He went.

Matthew 9:36 (NIV):

'When he saw the crowds, he had compassion on them, because they were harassed and helpless, like sheep without a shepherd.'

To properly get this picture painted by this verse, you should know that the relationship between a sheep and a shepherd is one of serious, non-negotiable dependence.

Spurgeon in Guzik's commentary[31] says that:

'Before a man can truly say, "the LORD is my shepherd," he must first feel himself to be a sheep by nature, "for he cannot know that God is his Shepherd unless he feels in himself that he has the nature of a sheep." He must relate to a sheep in its foolishness, its dependency, and in the warped nature of its will.'

---

[31] David Guzik, *Psalms 23 commentary: https://enduringword.com/bible-com mentary/psalm-23/*

Jesus felt compassion for this sheep without a shepherd. Imagine how they must have been heading for destruction. We are like sheep, by nature. To wander without our shepherd is fatal.

> 'A sheep, saith Aristotle, is a foolish and sluggish creature...aptest of anything to wander, though it feel no want, and unablest to return...a sheep can make no shift to save itself from tempests or inundation; there it stands and will perish, if not driven away by the shepherd.'
>
> - Trapp (*Guzik's commentary*).

But guess what, our weakness as sheep becomes our greatest strength when it leads us to our Shepherd.

Jesus has given us this same compassion, that the lost sheep, through us, may find their true Shepherd. We have this same ministry; we are capable of this same love! How? Through the Holy Spirit.

Romans 5:5 (NLT):

'...For we know how dearly God loves us, because he has given us the Holy Spirit to fill our hearts with his love.'

Since He has given us this ministry of reconciliation, we can stand in the gap, interceding for the lost ones.

2 Corinthians 5: 14, 18-20 (NIV):

14 'For CHRIST'S LOVE COMPELS US, because we are convinced that one died for all, and therefore all died.'

18 All this is from God, who reconciled us to himself through Christ and gave us the ministry of reconciliation:

19 that God was reconciling the world to himself in Christ, not counting people's sins against them. And he has committed to us the message of reconciliation.

20 We are therefore Christ's ambassadors, as though God were making his appeal through us. We implore you on Christ's behalf: Be reconciled to God.'

Take another look at **verse 14**, CHRIST'S LOVE COMPELS US! This same love that had Jesus moved to tears at the death of Lazarus (**John 11**) and to deep compassion when He saw the people like sheep without a shepherd (**Matthew 9**) is in you and me. This love COMPELS us; it drives us, urges us, moves us, and provokes us to do good works for the kingdom. This love is the foundation of our faith, *'For God so loved the world...' (John 3:16).*

By this love, you, too, can feel His burden and heaviness as you fellowship with Him and share in His ministry of reconciling the lost to the Father. **Verse 20.** above, says we act as **Christ's ambassadors, as though God pleads with the lost through us**. Through you, God appeals to the lost. Through your life, the sacrifice of Jesus becomes obvious and more people are reconciled with God.

Do you believe this? Then this promise is for you:

John 14:12 (NIV):

'Very truly I tell you, whoever believes in me will do the works I have been doing, and they will do even greater things than these, because I am going to the Father.'

Jesus sits at the right hand of God, but the Holy Spirit is INSIDE you. Look and see! Through Him, you can do greater works for God's kingdom. Remember that you may be in this world, but you are not of it, so you must adequately represent the actual place that you are from - HEAVEN. An ambassador in a foreign country does his best to paint his country in the best possible light to foreigners. The same is your task.

Heaven starts here

Heaven is not where you get to when you die, it is what happens when you accept Christ. God's glory is in you; Leon Morris, a Christian scholar has this to say about this glory:

> 'The glory will be revealed, not created. The implication is that it is already existent, but not apparent.'

God's glory rests on you. Heaven is inside you!

A Son of God

Romans 8:14 affirms our Sonship in Christ, **'For all those led by the Spirit are God's Sons.'** While many think that this can either be a pre-condition or requirement, I believe that it goes both ways. The Holy Spirit is the One who convicts a sinner of unbelief. Therefore, we follow His leading to repent and become the Sons of God. Afterward, He continues to lead us in righteousness and keep our paths straight.

Being the light is being a son and acting like it. The prodigal son forgot he was still a son, and he came back begging - while that remorse was necessary, it's what we sometimes do, even as certified children of God. You cannot settle for crumbs when your father has a feast prepared for you. Everything in this book is not for 'some' Christians. It is for YOU.

If no one was left out in the upper room as the Spirit was poured out, then neither should you be left out of what God is doing here through this book that is in your hands. Being rooted in Christ is a matter of constantly seeking and panting for the Lord. We like to refer to some Christians as 'God's favourites', but the ones you may perceive in this manner are those who have taken advantage of God's gracious offer and are intimate with Him.

Do you know? That man is not the only one suffering as a result of sin? Look around you, and you will see that the earth suffers too.

The Bible confirms in Romans 8:19-22 (NKJV) that:

19 'For the earnest expectation of the creation eagerly waits for the revealing of the sons of God.

20 For the creation was subjected to futility, not willingly, but because of Him who subjected it in hope;

21 because the creation itself also will be delivered from the bondage of corruption into the glorious liberty of the children of God.

22 For we know that the whole creation groans and labors with birth pangs together until now.'

Prophet Isaiah in the Scriptures **11: 6-9 (NKJV)**, tells of a time when:

6 'The wolf also shall dwell with the lamb, the leopard shall lie down with the young goat, the calf and the young lion and the fatling together; and a little child shall lead them.

7 The cow and the bear shall graze; their young ones shall lie down together; and the lion shall eat straw like the ox.

8 The nursing child shall play by the cobra's hole, and the weaned child shall put his hand in the viper's den.

9 They shall not hurt nor destroy in all My holy mountain, for the earth shall be full of the knowledge of the LORD as the waters cover the sea.'

That time starts now. We are the Sons of God that will show forth His glory. Jesus is the hope we have for this, that men will ultimately be redeemed. In **verse 23** of **Romans 8,** we see that through the Holy Spirit, we have but a little taste of this glory of what is to come. Isn't that amazing?!? Now we have received adoption **(Romans 8:15)** but in that time, we will be fully consummated and receive new bodies in Him.

This is what the end will look like for us.

1 Corinthians 15:51-58 (NIV):

51 'Listen, I tell you a mystery: We will not all sleep, but we will all be changed—

52 in a flash, in the twinkling of an eye, at the last trumpet. For the trumpet will sound, the dead will be raised imperishable, and we will be changed.

53 For the perishable must clothe itself with the imperishable, and the mortal with immortality.

54 When the perishable has been clothed with the imperishable, and the mortal with immortality, then the saying that is written will come true: "Death has been swallowed up in victory.

55 "Where, O death, is your victory?

Where, O death, is your sting?"

56 The sting of death is sin, and the power of sin is the law.

57 But thanks be to God! He gives us the victory through our Lord Jesus Christ.

58 Therefore, my dear brothers and sisters, stand firm. Let nothing move you. Always give yourselves fully to the work of the Lord, because you know that your labour in the Lord is not in vain.

Hallelujah!

Journal prompt:

In what ways can you shine brighter at work, in your relationships, etc?

Matthew 5:14 (KJV) -

'Ye are the light of the world. A city that is set on an hill cannot be hid.'

Confession: I am the light of the world. I am a city set on a hill that will not be hidden. I shine as Jesus shines. My light reveals the darkness in the hearts of men and leads them to reconciliation with Abba—in Jesus' Name. Amen.

What's on your mind? What does being a light mean to you now? Are you burning with excitement on how to take this world for God? Take a minute to say a prayer and write down the ideas and thoughts that come to your mind as you pray in the spirit.

_____

_____

_____

_____

_____

_____

_____

_____

_____

_____

_____

_____

_____

_____

_____

_____

_____

_____

13

Is Purpose...?

2 Timothy 1:9 (NIV) - *'who has saved us and called us with a holy calling, not according to our works, but according to His own purpose and grace which was granted us in Christ Jesus from all eternity,'*

The Talk of Purpose, *'what am I supposed to be doing here?'* is as old as humanity, itself. And why not? The Bible, itself, tells us that God prepared us in advance for *'good works'* (**Ephesians 2:10**). Before we go any further, I want to let you know that there is one purpose of man on earth - no matter the channel through which it is undertaken - and it is to glorify God. **Revelations 4:11** clarifies that God created everything He created for His pleasure.

Revelations 4:11 (NIV):

"You are worthy, our Lord and God,

to receive glory and honour and power,

for you created all things,

and by your will they were created

and have their being."

Now to break it down, everyone still has that unique talent that makes them stand out from the next person, thus the constant clamour for purpose. What is your purpose? What unique thing do you bring to the table?

There are certain things you must know as we proceed on this Talk of Purpose:

1. **Purpose is not a destination.** We often think that purpose is that *one thing* you are supposed to do all the days of your life, but it is rarely that. Your purpose is to follow God's lead to all the places He wants you to be.

2. **There is a need for active waiting on God to reveal His specific purpose for you.** While every believer has the responsibility of the Great Commission (**Matthew 28:19-20**), to carry the Gospel to the ends of the earth, there are different ways - distinct to the talents and abilities - that God has given us by which God will have us carry out this responsibility. The body of Christ is diverse and all parts work together for the good of the collective body (**1 Corinthians 12:27-30**). Therefore, as you share the Gospel, carry out the Great Commission, and be the Light, loving God and the people He created, you must actively ask God what He will have you do, how you can

use your *unique* talents for the Gospel. Ask, *'How can I contribute to Your kingdom agenda, Jesus?'* *'What can I start to push the Gospel further?'* *'How can I bring God to my street, my local community, or my industry?'* *'What can I build for the church?'* God is always seeking for people to stand in the gap in different places as the need arises. God is always looking for people to send to do His work **(Isaiah 6:8)**. *God is looking for you.*

3. **Your talents are often a good pointer to what your purpose is: '*What is in your hand?*' (Exodus 4:2)** is a good pointer to what unique gift you have. However, the danger of overreliance on such a talent remains, so we must always be open to God's leading. Do not hold on too tightly to your talent that you are uncomfortable and unwilling to step out of your comfort zone. The worst thing is to succeed in a place you are not meant to be. **Designation is not always the destination**. Read that again. And again.

4. **Fulfilling purpose takes proven character,** which we need to build up because God not only wants to take us to great heights, He wants us to be able to maintain them. There is a process **(Romans 5:3),** and we must appreciate the process that God is taking time to put us through. Like a refining fire **(Mark 9:49). Deuteronomy 8** tells us that God took the Israelites through the wilderness to test their ability to remain faithful without becoming prideful. How can you be faithful in big things if

you are not in small ones? **(Luke 16:10)**. David was a musician in the palace before he became a king in the palace. The things that you desire are attached to a version of you that does not exist yet. You must become that version of you to be able to properly manage the resources or carry out the instructions that God will give. Do you really think you can handle it if God tells you exactly what He wants you to do, without following due process? Then consider Jonah, who got swallowed by a fish as a consequence of trying to subvert God's process because he did not want to follow through with it. Do not be in a hurry. Go through the process.

5. **Purpose does not revolve around you:** Purpose revolves around God, the Giver of Purpose. It is not about you but about how your life can impact the lives of others. When we declare that the Gospel prevails, for example, it is through our hands! That is the purpose. It prevails in whatever aspect of life or field that you may find yourself in. You can take your industry or that mountain of influence, whether it be education or entertainment, for God.

I want to hammer on point number 2 because I have seen it repeatedly happen, where people simply wait instead of doing what they can, given the situation. Consider the parable of the talents **(Matthew 25:14-30)**, where the last servant refused to do *nada*[32] with what he was given. Now, realise it was barely about the amount of the talents or how we often perceive God as unfair in His dissemination of resources but the unwillingness to move with what we have. That is simply being an ingrate no matter how you want to look at it.

Do you know? Even if you use your talents for evil, it is better than lack of use because, through misuse, you can often discover the correct use. However, no such thing can happen in lack of use. Furthermore, not doing what you should do, as a believer, signifies unbelief. If you do believe, you will do it. Works prove faith.

James 2:26 (NLT):

'Just as the body is dead without breath, so also faith is dead without good works.'

If your purpose is truly to glorify God, you should be less bothered about trying to stand out or make a name for yourself and more concerned about giving glory to God. The irony is that God always glorifies the one who glorifies Him; see this in the life of Jesus; Abraham, sacrificing his son; the chronicle of David and Goliath, and others.

You do not live for yourself. You are a soldier in God's army by default, and it is not optional for some Christians to spread the Gospel and others not to. That's a lie from the pit of hell. Evangelism is

---

[32] nothing

not an offer or a contract that you can accept or decline. **2 Timothy 2:4** posits that a soldier only thinks of pleasing his Commander. You are that soldier. There is a bandwagon of Christians who believe that salvation is truly personal to the point that they do not need to evangelise or spread the Gospel. If you have read this book, at all, then you know that is untrue. If you do not spread the Gospel, how will the unsaved hear? **(Romans 10:17)**.

You are a disciple-making disciple. You are more than enough. The only thing you need to preach the Gospel is the Gospel that saved you. If the Bible instructs that we must be ready to give a response for the hope in us **(1 Peter 3:15)**, then it means that each person that possesses this faith has a responsibility to share and defend it.

1 Peter 3:15 (NLT):

'Instead, you must worship Christ as Lord of your life. And if someone asks about your hope as a believer, always be ready to explain it.'

No, you are not perfect, but God knew that when He imputed righteousness to you and did not make you earn it - because you simply cannot. All you need to do is continuously strive, press on as you lay aside every sin that so easily besets you **(Philippians 3:14; Hebrews 12:1),** and grow in sanctification.

Many times, you will just be the right person at the right place to share Jesus. You are not unqualified; you are more than qualified. You have what makes you special: unique talents, gifts, abilities to serve people with; your unique perspective to meeting Jesus! You have a story only you can tell and invite people to. You are all Jesus needs. It is you He wants to go get the one with. You are His love letter to people.

You are enough. Just be you. And all things will work together, the Bible in **Romans 8:28** lets us know this. But this is not restricted to the usual narrow idea of a one-thing-to-do-for-God kind of purpose. It is every part of your life. Nothing is isolated from God.

Do you know *what* Purpose is? Purpose is God. He is the One that makes everything else matter.

02/09/2021

'DO NOT ATTEMPT TO HIDE WHAT I'M DOING THROUGH YOU.'

I hear these words from the Holy Spirit while praying. They speak deeply to me; me who - not intentionally but at this point - is hiding God. I have thought being trivial about the things of God in public is cool as long as I take Him seriously in private. How could I? How can you hide light?

I say the same words to you today: do not attempt to hide what God is doing through you in any sphere. Do not think of it as too little. Greater works you will do by the Spirit, with the greatest motive of the glorification of Jesus!

I resonate with this quote by Brother Lawrence in Practice The Presence of God[33]. He said:

> 'That we ought not to be weary of doing little things for the love of GOD, who regards not the greatness of the work, but the love with which it is performed.'

Please pray this with me:

> *I have found this treasure and I am keeping it.*
>
> *I'll give my life if I have to.*
>
> *Nothing makes sense without You.*
>
> *I will be living my life according to this truth.*
>
> *You are the One we have repeatedly stood up and yet You have not stood up.*
>
> *You have not left the room. You're too merciful!*
>
> *Thank You for this grace. Empower me as I go out to do Your will.*
>
> *For greater is You in me, than he that is in the world.*
>
> *in Jesus' Name*
>
> Amen.

---

[33] The Practice of the Presence of God is a book of collected teachings of Brother Lawrence, a 17th-century Carmelite friar, compiled by Father Joseph de Beaufort. First published in 1692.

Journal prompt:

Exhale and ponder over what you just read. What is that thing that you have always felt was your singular purpose in God? How does it connect to the Gospel?

2 Timothy 1:9 (NIV) -

'Who has saved us and called us with a holy calling, not according to our works, but according to His own purpose and grace which was granted us in Christ Jesus from all eternity,'

Confession: I declare my life is aligned with God's purpose for me. I am only what God has called me to be and nothing more. My talents, gifts and calling all work together for the love and glory of God—in Jesus' Name. Amen.

What is your purpose in Christ? How do your talent, dreams or what you currently do relate with the Gospel? If they don't, how can they?

14

My Secret Place

James 4:8 (NLT) - *'Come close to God, and God will come close to you.'*

10/05/2022

Dear Abba,

I cannot believe how much I have grown in You, how You have helped me mature. I cannot believe how You answer the prayers I forgot that I prayed. I cannot comprehend how You took my hand to write this book. How people help me for no reason. May my heart always be where You want it to be.

I remember being scared when my dreams started to come alive in You; how could I not be? All I had were my dreams, but You told me they were not going to stay in my head. You were going to make them tangible, and You did. I love how I am learning to see people through Your eyes. I am growing into Your soldier.

Lord, how do You help me so much? You outdo Yourself every day. You never let me wallow. You pick me up and put me on my feet. You give me the things I need before I know that I need them. My life is so beautiful and it is because of You.

Abba, thank You.

•••

I write letters to God, sometimes they're long and sometimes they are short. I believe it - writing letters to God - comes naturally to me because of my inky ability. It's also how I dwell in my secret place, the presence of God - by writing love letters to Him.

This may be the most important chapter of this book, but I will leave it to you to decide.

Before I got saved, I was a mess. Now when people hear me say this, they think I must be exaggerating but the reality that people see is often very different from the truth. When I got saved, I dived headfirst into God's embrace. It was like drinking water, cold water, after walking in the desert for days. More like years.

It is the best decision I have ever made.

At the start of my journey, I made many silly mistakes, which I will not share, here, for the sake of decorum. However, what constantly saved me from making costly mistakes was the fact that I ALWAYS went back to God. No matter what my pastor shared in church or what a Christian influencer advocates for, I would never let it rest in my heart until I had it approved by my spirit. With my spirit now connected to the Holy Spirit, I was in sure hands.

Where am I going with this? My friend, you will come across many light bearers - like you - who mean well and want to impart the knowledge of God to you, especially through their experiences. However, you may apply such knowledge in error if you do not make it a habit to court the presence of God. You are at a particular place in your Christian journey, different from many other people, the Holy Spirit is your only surest lead.

We often make the mistake of inheriting not just the Word but the unintentional biases or patterns of those who preach it and adopting those models as all-encompassing and right. For example, it is easy to think that your church is the only church that is getting it right because your pastor preaches so eloquently but the other church you attended, the pastor stammers. Well guess what? Moses was a stammerer **(Exodus 4:10-17)** and God could have cured him but instead, Aaron stood in as his (Moses') mouthpiece! Your pastor may dress very nicely but guess what? John the Baptist **'wore clothing made of camel's hair, with a leather belt around his waist, and he ate locusts and wild honey' (Mark 1:6, NIV).** THE WORD IS THE MODEL OF YOUR FAITH, NOT A HUMAN BEING!

God's calling on your life is distinct and it is His lead that you must follow, not pre-established patterns set by human beings. Don't limit God because you have a limited idea of what He can do based on what you have seen in the lives of other Christians or ministries. What if God wants you to be the first of many? There is no impossibility with Him.

This is why you must KNOW God for yourself and let the Word be your foundation. Embrace the Holy Spirit, however He chooses to move in your life. Many experiences, testimonies and miracles from other people may assure you of the reality and truth of God but only personal knowledge and conviction will keep you aligned in His will for you and see you through to the very end.

Many times, when people falter in their walk with God, it can be traced to weak personal conviction.

Matthew 16:13-17 (NLT):

13 'When Jesus came to the region of Caesarea Philippi, he asked his disciples, "Who do people say that the Son of Man is?"

14 "Well," they replied, "some say John the Baptist, some say Elijah, and others say Jeremiah or one of the other prophets."

15 Then he asked them, "But who do you say I am?"

16 Simon Peter answered, "You are the Messiah, the Son of the living God."

17 Jesus replied, "You are blessed, Simon son of John, because my Father in heaven has revealed this to you. You did not learn this from any human being.'

Jesus is less interested in what you have heard other people say He is, He wants to know who you say that He is! Like **verse 17** insists, such knowledge cannot be learnt from any human being, nobody can tell you who God is for you. Only God can reveal Himself, His truth, to you. This is personal conviction.

This truth can only be revealed to you in the secret place. The secret place is where you go to meet with God; at the door, you leave behind every fear, anxiety, worry or wrong beliefs. And when you come out, those things you left behind will not be waiting any longer. The secret place is the secret behind every great man or woman of God.

Dwelling in God constantly helped me grow rapidly in the knowledge of the things of the kingdom. As a believer, God puts a yearning in your heart for Him. When you ask God to *'try you by fire'* or *'use you,'* I hope you know that He will, but it is really up to you to succumb to that yearning and actually take action. Nevertheless, God's mercy always comes through even at the times that we do not.

Take it from me, following God's leading will save you a lot of stress. Like, God already has everything figured out, all you have to do is obey! Easier said than done, maybe, but that is why we have the Holy Spirit.

I will give you an instance of how God's leading in my life has been superb as a result of my dwelling.

When God reminded me that I was to write a book, I said 'Yes Sir,' and continued with everything else except the book. It was not that I did not want to do it but I just had a lot going on. Not only did God remind me through my close friend, the week after, He supplied the name of the book. The way it happened was so funny, I was having a conversation with my friend, Elvis, in a car as we were on our way somewhere and I randomly said it. However, I heard a *zing*[34] in my spirit immediately and I just *knew*. My spirit was able to recognize God through that very 'ordinary' situation.

It may shock you to know that this was not the book I set out to write. But on the very day God gave me the name of this book, I began. From there, it was something amazing watching God write through me. It was (is) an honour. When I finished writing this book and read through it, I could not believe God could use me in this way. I remember telling Amanda that it felt like I was reading someone else's book. Must be the Holy Spirit.

The truth of the life that I live now is that I sought after God and He gave me everything I ever wanted. All I did was follow and it was not like I was a pro at following, but God not only tells you what to do, He goes along with you to do it.

One discipline that has changed my life is that every morning, I plan out my day with God. Spending time with God, learning of Him, will build your trust beyond what you can ever imagine. You will become like Jesus, who could sleep even when the storm was raging all around Him.

I figure out my life as I dwell in the secret place. God tells my spirit what to do. He gives me the best ideas in work, business, relationships... everything! I literally never pray without a jotter or the Notes app on my phone. As a new believer, I used to expect God to speak in very obvious ways and He did. Growing up, I just *know*

---

[34] depiction of a eureka moment

things in my spirit and act on them and they turn out right. This is because the Spirit of God is within me and His influence on my spirit makes it possible for me to truly trust my heart on anything and not be led astray.

I have said all this to say that PAPA IS THE COOLEST. God will really *baby* you if you come to Him and you will mature eventually. You rarely have the strength to do what God has asked you to do but once you say YES, you will receive strength from above. God has *babied* me and when I remember the many times I cried because of a decision-making process He helped me through, I feel so embarrassed because why was I even crying? *cringe.*

I used to bear the nickname *'Rehdwolf,'* and on the day God told me I had to let the name go, I threw a tantrum and shed hot tears. After He explained to me why the name had to go, I understood but I still did not have a replacement. That same day, He supplied it. I repeat, God will *baby* you. He is your Father and when you lack the maturity in many areas, be assured He will softly guide you through them.

When you dwell in the secret place, God will become the most important thing in your life. It will be so easy for you to be unattached to anything in this world. I remember once in university when God told me, clearly, to empty my Piggy Flex and give it to Him. *I wan mad*[35]. I hesitated; I would go broke if I did it. But I would not have peace of mind if I did not, so I did. I made sure that as much as I could, disobeying God was never an option.

---

[35] Nigerian Pidgin English for I went berserk

I entered the app, initiated a withdrawal but got notified that I had withdrawn my maximum and would have to wait - I didn't even know there was such a thing as a maximum limit until that Sunday morning. Immediately I saw that notification, I heard God tell me *'Well done'* in my spirit. I knew I had passed His test. He did not want my money; He wanted my obedience. What an expensive (literally) joke, Lord.

The secret place turns your heart to where it should be. Many times, I have embarked on a fast to pray about certain things but at the end of each fast, I end up embracing the will of God. He literally turns my face away from those things and says, *'No, Favour, look at me instead; I AM the wealth you should be seeking.'*

In life, there are situations in which you prevail and there are others that you must flee. You will be able to pick your battles with wisdom when you dwell. The secret place increases your ability to yield to the Holy Spirit within you as you come into the knowledge of Him. When you surrender, when you get out of the way, then God can really do His thing. The end of man is the beginning of God, as a popular quote says.

> 'When man works, man works
> When man prays, God works'
>
> - Unknown

Every time I pray, I ask God to search my heart, the Psalmist's prayer in **Psalm 139: 23-24.**

Psalms 139:23-24 (NLT):

'Search me, O God, and know my heart;

test me and know my anxious thoughts.

Point out anything in me that offends you,

and lead me along the path of everlasting life.'

This prayer is so necessary because we often hold things in our heart and we fail to realise this unless God reveals it to us. Sin separates us from God but with this prayer, the Holy Spirit reveals our offences to us and we confess them.

The secret place is for you. All you have to do is follow God. All you have to do is return when you fall. **The secret place is where you find strength in a time of weakness.**

Come to the secret place. Remain there. Build intimacy with God and His presence will follow you even when your knees are not kissing the ground or your head, bowed. God's presence is not a place like church or your prayer room, it is a consciousness that you carry with you. The secret place is within you.

Remember, the wisest proverbs in the book of Proverbs says:

Proverbs 3:5-6 (KJV):

5 'Trust in the LORD with all thine heart; And lean not unto thine own understanding.

6 In all thy ways acknowledge him, And he shall direct thy paths.'

In ALL your ways, do not think you know better. If you try to autopilot with God, you will crash. Dwell in the secret place, let God be your first resort and not last.

The result? Your life will be a testimony of what happens when a man trusts God wholly. The secret place is for you and Abba. So dwell.

Journal prompt:

How intimate are you with God? Do you take out time to simply focus on Him? Let's practise - You can write Him a letter, a song; you can sing or even stay listening. Simply give Him your full attention and you can progress from there, worshipping and adoring Him every moment of the day.

James 4:8 (NLT) -

'Come close to God, and God will come close to you.'

Confession: I confess that You are all that matters to me and this will show henceforth in my devotion to You, Abba. I have time for You, I give my best time to You. You will never have to compete - with the things You have given me - for my attention. I am Yours and You are mine. I will forever be in this secret place as I carry You with me.

Write a love letter to Abba. Be as expressive as you can be, He longs to hear from you.

15

Little Children

1 **John 5:21 (NIV)** - *'Little children, keep yourselves from idols.'*

To be light means you are plugged in. To remain a light means that you stay connected to your source. You are a son.

Idols go beyond what we see with our eyes; they are (any and all) things that attempt to take the glory away from God. This temptation will occur, I promise you, but you must flee from it. There is this thing that I do to redirect glory to God; whenever anyone tells me *'Thank you'* for anything that I do, I quickly interject *'Bless God.'* It may seem unnecessary but it helps me to externalise such thanks. As it should be.

I love how **NLT** puts it:

1 John 5:21:

"Dear children, keep away from anything that might take God's place in your hearts."

Notice the 'might,' it suggests that you flee from even the appearance of evil. Don't wait to be certain; If it *looks like* it will take glory from God, if it *looks like* it will lead you to sin, you are not wrong to flee.

In positions of power or influence - in fact, in everyday ordinary life, there will be temptations to take this glory. Consider Jesus, David and many other patriarchs like Daniel and the fire boys in Babylon. In fact, people will see God's power working through you and may attempt to worship you in some way **(Acts 14:11-13)**. Remember who the glory belongs to. Our Lord of the Armies is a jealous God and rightly so, who are you to claim glory for His power?

Here is a profound example from the Bible:

Acts 14:8-15 (NIV):

8 'In Lystra there sat a man who was lame. He had been that way from birth and had never walked.

9 He listened to Paul as he was speaking. Paul looked directly at him, saw that he had faith to be healed

10 and called out, "Stand up on your feet!" At that, the man jumped up and began to walk.

11 When the crowd saw what Paul had done, they shouted in the Lycaonian language, "The gods have come down to us in human form!"

12 Barnabas they called Zeus, and Paul they called Hermes because he was the chief speaker.

13 The priest of Zeus, whose temple was just outside the city, brought bulls and wreaths to the city gates because he and the crowd wanted to offer sacrifices to them.

14 But when the apostles Barnabas and Paul heard of this, they tore their clothes and rushed out into the crowd, shouting:

15 "Friends, why are you doing this? We too are only human, like you. We are bringing you good news, telling you to turn from these worthless things to the living God, who made the heavens and the earth and the sea and everything in them.'

I was relatively a babe in Christ when one time, a person wanted to pay his tithe to me because he received a miracle after I prayed for him. It was incredible to me (and I got scared because it opened my eyes to something I had no idea of before) but I refused it. I saw no need for it. It often starts this way if one is not careful. Once, it took a close friend for me to realise I was starting to focus more on the numbers from social media rather than what actually mattered. Don't take the glory meant for God. Walk in the Spirit, and you will not fulfil the desires of the flesh **(Galatians 5:16).**

A key to keeping the glory for God is hidden in plain sight in the Scripture.

1 John 2:15 - 16 (KJV) says:

15 'Love not the world, neither the things that are in the world. If any man love the world, the love of the Father is not in him.

16 For all that is in the world, the lust of the flesh, and the lust of the eyes, and the pride of life, is not of the Father, but is of the world.'

Love not this world! He that loves his life will lose it and vice versa **(John 12:25)**. To live for God means to take up your cross daily, deny yourself and follow God **(Matthew 16:24)**. Eyes on the prize, my friend.

If it is any encouragement, what you may perceive as the greatest thing God has done for you is merely a part of the whole that He wants to commit into your hands. What often prompts a man redirecting God's glory to himself is the gifts of God, but those blessings and prosperity that we may let get to our heads are barely a tip of the iceberg. If you are swayed by a little influence, how can He commit even greater ones into your hands?

Remember to LET God, it is He who IS working in you - both to will and to work according to His good purpose. **(Philippians 2:13)**. He is doing all the heavy lifting. Just yield. God is not just our end, He's our means too.

Little children, keep yourselves from idols.

Journal prompt:

What often takes away your attention from God? What steps can you take to stop it? Head to your journal and take the first step to pray Psalms 139, May God reveal your idols to you even as He takes them away.

1 John 5:21 (NIV):

'Little children, keep yourselves from idols.'

Confession: I declare that I am exempt(ed) from everything that attempts to take the glory from God. I flee from every temptation and I am helped by the Spirit, my Helper, who lives in me. The light that is Jesus lives in me and God's love guides my every move and thought and word. Above all, my life - in action or inaction - gives God utmost glory—in Jesus' Name. Amen.

*Write out **Psalms 139: 23-24.** What often takes away your attention from God? What steps can you take to stop it?*

_____

_____

_____

_____

_____

_____

_____

_____

_____

_____

_____

_____

_____

_____

_____

_____

_____

_____

_____

_____

A Last Word

ABBA's light,

This is my labour of love for you and by God, I will labour more and often. Don't forget to always come back here to document your progress; I am not only rooting for you but I am praying ceaselessly for you.

(insert your name), you start to function as Light. May you lead thousands and millions to reconciliation with Abba. May His perfect grace and mercy keep you and those around you. Above all, may the Lamb receive the reward of His sacrifice in your life. In Jesus' Name. Amen.

> **Philippians 2:15 (NLT):**
>
> **'...Live clean, innocent lives as children of God, shining like bright lights in a world full of crooked and perverse people.'**

Where light goes, darkness disappears.

Shalom.

From the Author

Thank you for reading this book, thank you. Before this book got into your hands, I prayed for you. I prayed that I would not get in the way and neither would you but that the Holy Spirit would work His mighty power in our lives to bring about change through love.

I hope this book changes your life the way it did mine. I would love to hear from you too, questions, contributions, testimonies - everything! You can connect with me by scanning the QR code below.

https://natha.ng/my-library/

See you in my next book.
God bless you.

Extracts

All the responsibilities that come with being the light - Instagram post on @Maranatha.__ on 21/11/2021.

All the responsibilities that come with being the light of the world

A countless number of times I have declared, as I am sure you have as well, that:

'I am the light of the world, a city set on a hill cannot be hid.' (Matthew 5:14). But what does this even mean?

We'll start from the functions of light:

- Light guides
- Light separates
- Light protects
- Light attracts

How does light guide?

I'll explain with this - if you've watched any movies about ships or a shipwreck, there's always mention of a lighthouse. The lighthouse functions to guide ships that have lost their way at sea. With the light, these ships can easily find their way back to the right path by fixing their eyes on the light. As Christians, our light shines so children of God who have lost their way can be reconciled to the Father.

How does light separate?

Imagine it's really dark outside, it's like 12am at dawn, but there is power (light) in your house so it's okay. There's a separation. But then suddenly, NEPA (the power holding company) performs magic and the light goes off. What separates you from the darkness outside? Nothing. That is how light separates. The distinction between light and darkness is so strong that when you were inside your house with light, you couldn't even put a finger on the darkness around you. Heaven, you barely even notice it.

As Christians, we should be that light; that separating energy. That when people come close to us, they can feel a contrast in energy and in a good way that makes them think. I don't know what this person has but I want to be around them as much as possible.

How does light protect?

In horror movies that I have watched, when a group of people are under attack, they always want to be where the light is. The reason is not far-fetched: in the light, you're safe.

Not coincidentally, when there is about to be an attack, the first thing that happens is that the light goes off. Darkness cannot flourish where there is light, that's how light protects. As Christians? Our light should protect those around us and even further, as much as we can. We pray for not just ourselves but our families, our friends and even our enemies.

Finally, how does light attract?

I'll illustrate with this; why do fair people seem more attractive?

They might not necessarily be relatively beautiful but we always find our eyes drawn to look at them. That is the power of light. We can't help but look at it. We can't help but be drawn to it. It automatically catches our attention. At least physically.

Spiritually, Jesus makes our lives beautiful by default and this stands us out.

People are attracted to this beauty and v16 of Matthew 5 says,

"Let your light so shine that men may see your good deeds and glorify your Father who is in heaven.'

People see us and they want to know the reason behind the shine. It's God.

As Christians, we must be intentional about our light. Just like we place the light in the ceiling and not on the ground or a lamp on a table where it can give the most light, we must seek to amplify our light as much as we can so it spreads and shines in broader ways.

Shalom.

World people;

10/04/2022 - *Blog post excerpt from Natha.ng*
I am at a friend's get together for his birthday and it is far from a Christian hangout. In fact, world people are the ones here. The last time I was in a gathering like this, I cannot remember.

I feel the usual response gathering moss within me; to stay taciturn? Or to open my mouth and socialise? I pick the latter. Thankfully, the Holy Spirit was in charge and I went with Amanda so it was a form of accountability.

We Christians often run away from the ones we should be evangelising to. I do not advocate being evenly yoked with an unbeliever or regularly going to places with plenty of world people - especially if you do not have the maturity for it. However, you must have the mindset that each person is simply a person that needs the love of God and is deserving of His mercy. If you can see people the way that God sees them, you will relate in the manner that shows this - Christian or world gathering.

If you do end up in such a place or group of people, do not hide your light. You are there for a reason. Seek God's glorification. At the event I cited above, we were playing a game where I was asked to sing my favourite song and I sang *Jireh* by Maverick City. My friend was asked where she had experienced the most growth this year and she said it was in her relationship with God. Those were proud moments for us; showing off our Abba. Who knows who was watching? Who knows who we encouraged by our boldness?

If people gather for an agenda not of God, it is a soul winning opportunity for you. Your light will shine and the darkness will comprehend it not (John 1:5).

Satan go confuse[36].

Mirror Mirror

23/05/2022 - *Blog post excerpt from Natha.ng*

In the beginning, God made man in His image (Gen 1:26), we know that. Think about it, when Adam conversed with God in the cool of the evening, He must have looked upon the face of a God no different from himself. Adam looked like God.

Then sin happened and that image got distorted. God being a Holy God could not stand sin, thus causing a strain in the relationship between man and God. Can you still be close to one that your eyes cannot behold? The effect of sin triggered endless catastrophe.

'Your eyes are too pure to look on evil.'

Habakkuk 1:3

Sin made it possible to look at God, who we should look like, and see a total stranger; one with whom we should have all things in common but now have nothing in common. Through sin, the bond between ourselves and our significant other, Abba, seemed to be lost.

---

[36] Nigerian Pidgin expression loosely translated as The enemy will be confused

But Jesus came and if it is true that 'Jesus is the express image of God,' (Hebrews 1:3), it means that men were once again confronted with the reality and possibility of our real nature, the true nature of God in us. It means that in the eyes of Jesus, men could see the truth of who they were meant to be. It means that the cloak of sin could be peeled away to slowly but surely reveal the Adam that God initially created.

The sacrifice of Jesus, asides from atoning for our sins, also provided a classical example of the possibility - that if God could come down as a man and live without sin through the power of the Holy Spirit then so can we. Besides, '... we do not have a high priest who is unable to empathise with our weaknesses, but we have one who has been tempted in every way, just as we are—yet he did not sin.' (Hebrews 4:15).

Despite sin, we can still accept salvation bought through the blood of Jesus and slowly but surely get to the point where we look more and more like Him, just like we are supposed to.

I love 2 Corinthians 3:18 so much. Here is what it says:

But we all, with open face beholding as in a glass the glory of the Lord, are changed into the same image from glory to glory, even as by the Spirit of the Lord.

You see that! I want to let you know that as a believer, the more you spend time with God, the more you are changed into the same image. You begin to look more and more like Him, just like you were initially made to.

'And have put on the new man, which is renewed in knowledge after the image of him that created him.'

Colossians 3:10

Notice something important in the above verse, the new man which is your real nature in God, is renewed through your knowledge of God. It means that the more you study God's Word, the more you unlock new facets of your identity in Christ.

I have watched countless cartoons or movies where the hero was abandoned from birth and is probably getting trained by a guardian in order to come into his real power. The more he is exposed to the knowledge of who he truly is, the more he can harness his power.

The more you look into God's Word, the more you discover your true identity in God. That, in itself, is POWER. And why not? When the people of God daily perish literally because of lack of knowledge. If you never know what you can do, what is possible, then you may never try to do it. Lack of knowledge is a limitation.

'And to put on the new self, created after the likeness of God in true righteousness and holiness.'

Ephesians 4:24

The life given to us by Christ is one that looks like God, so when we become born again that is who we become. We are set apart for Holy works! However, we must intentionally study God's word to harness the power that He has deposited in us. We must look at

Jesus (the Word in flesh) and often, to discern the truth about our birth and origin. Our purpose, if you may.

Mirror mirror, is no longer on the wall
It is right in your hands
This mirror looks beyond the cloak of your skin
This mirror sees straight into your heart
This mirror is the Bible.

Shalom.

About the Author

Maranatha (Favour Nnaemeka) is an evangelist whose yielding to God's call upon her life has blessed many people. She currently stewards a Christian community called Jars of Clay, where she helps believers gain a strong footing in their walk with Christ. She also runs a blog, Natha.ng, where she shares struggles in her Walk of Faith while inspiring through stories and a mailing list where she shares weekly, intimate letters to help people come closer to God and be reminded that The Lord is Coming. She is the author of *The Devotional Cheat Code*, a Christian guide to maintaining consistency in their walk with God. This is her second published book.